Air Fryer Cookbook for Beginners

Dive into Crispy, Delicious Delights and Bid Farewell to Soggy Microwaved and Oven-Reheated Meals [IV EDITION]

Copyright © 2023

Sarah Roslin

COPYRIGHT & DISCLAIMER: all rights are reserved by law. No part of this book can be reproduced without the author's written permission. It is expressly forbidden to transmit this book to others, either in paper or electronic format, neither for money nor free of charge. What is reported in this book is the result of years of studies and accumulated experience. The achievement of the same results is not guaranteed. The reader assumes full responsibility for their choices. The book is exclusively for educational purposes.

TABLE OF CONTENTS

1	INTRODUCTION	3
2	QUICK & EASY RECIPES	11
3	FISH & SEAFOOD RECIPES	21
4	VEGETARIAN PLATE RECIPES	29
5	VEGAN PLATE RECIPES	37
6	SIDE DISH RECIPES	45
7	POULTRY RECIPES	50
8	PORK RECIPES	58
9	BEEF RECIPES	63
10	LAMB RECIPES	68
11	DESSERT RECIPES	73
12	SNACK & APPETIZER RECIPES	78
13	MEAL PLAN	88
13	ANALYTICAL INDEX	102
14	CONCLUSION	104
15	BONUS	104
16	ANNEX – A	105
17	ANNEX - B	106
18	FAQS	107
19	MEASUREMENTS	108

1 INTRODUCTION

In the evolving culinary landscape, the quest for healthier yet delectable cooking methods has ushered in the age of the air fryer. A staple in modern kitchens, this nifty gadget is more than just a trend—it's a culinary revolution. Whether it landed on your countertop as a thoughtful gift or a spontaneous purchase, you're on the brink of a transformative cooking experience. The air fryer, with its unique air-cooking mechanism, not only drastically reduces the caloric content usually introduced by fats and oils but also guarantees a golden crispness that accentuates the natural flavors. Dive into the "Air Fryer Cookbook" and embark on a journey of flavorful, crispy, and healthier culinary delights!

1.1 Air Fryer: Crispy Delights, Less Oil

We've already mentioned that an air fryer is a kitchen appliance that cooks your foods in air rather than oil and fat. Cooking in an air fryer is cleaner, easier, and healthier than using a deep fat fryer. When you taste air-fried foods, you'll notice the difference. They have an authentic, home-cooked taste to them, with a fresh crunch to everything. For the most part, you simply need to add your ingredients to your air fryer in the recipe order and follow the instructions. All air flyers are easy to use and once you understand the features of your particular model, there'll be no stopping you. It's a good idea to ensure that you keep your air fryer out on your kitchen countertop and don't use it once or twice and then store it in the cupboard. There is an 'out of sight, out of mind' problem with all kitchen appliances and you might not get the best use out of it if it's not easily accessible. By having your air fryer within easy reach, you can use it daily to create delicious breakfasts, lunches, dinners, desserts, and even snacks. It's a truly versatile machine that will surprise you with its never-ending options.

1.2 Air Fryer: Why It's a Culinary Game-Changer

You only have to do a quick online search for kitchen appliances, and you'll find all manner of gadgets on sale. Some are good, some are not so good. So, what sets an air fryer apart and makes it one of those things that you just have to invest in?

We've already mentioned that air fryers are easy to use and make your food taste great, but let's outline a list here so you can see the benefits of using an air fryer regularly.

- Air fryers are very easy to use
- Different models have a range of different features
- Ideal for busy lifestyles as your food will be cooked quickly
- Foods are cooked in air, which cuts down on the amount of oil you consume daily
- Your foods will be crispier and fresher
- Streamlined versions are easy to leave on your countertop and easy to store away when necessary
- Modern appliances are easy to clean, and some parts can even be washed in a dishwasher (always check your particular appliance instructions to be sure this is the case for your model)
- A huge number of recipes can be created in your air fryer - more than you know right now!

It's vital that you do your homework when purchasing an air fryer and shop around. You'll find many different models on the market, and it pays to ensure that you're purchasing an appliance that will suit your needs. When you're looking to buy an air fryer, these are the things you really need to keep in mind:

Air fryer capacity - All air fryers have a different capacity in terms of how much food you can cook inside them at any time. If you have a large family, you'll need a bigger capacity, which will probably have a larger price tag. However, if it's only 1-4 people in your household, you can probably get away with a regular-sized air fryer.

Your budget - Don't splurge a huge amount of cash on an air fryer with a million features you will not use. Identify your budget and find an air fryer that falls within that range.

Different features - Yes, you don't need an all singing, all dancing appliance, but do some research into the various features available and choose the ones that are important to you. This will inform your purchasing decision.

Make and guarantee - When you buy anything from a big brand name, you usually feel more confident that you're getting quality and that it will last. If this is important to you, go for a big name in the kitchen appliance world. Also, ensure you get at least a year's guarantee with your appliance, which is usually the case.

1.3 Oil Fried Food Vs. Air Fried Foods

We know that air fryers cook your food in air, not oil, as a typical deep-fat fryer would. If you use a regular frying pan or deep fat fryer, add some heat able oil to the pan and cook the food. The issue here is that the ingredients you add to the pan or fryer soak up some of that oil, creating a different texture and, in most cases, adding to the calorie and fat content of the food you're cooking. The other problem with cooking in oil is that you need to be extremely careful, as it's easy for 'spits' of oil to fly out of the pan, burning anyone standing too close. Of course, improper supervision of oil frying can also result in fires in some cases. While frying fat foods tends to work out cheaper, the ever-rising cost of purchasing oil means that an air fryer will probably pay for itself over time. You will save on buying oil and pay for the electricity your air fryer needs to turn on and create energy. Electric isn't particularly low-cost these days either. However, modern air fryers are pretty energy efficient, and the amount of electricity this type of device uses is relatively low, especially compared to older models. For that reason, consider the energy efficiency rating when purchasing an air fryer and choose accordingly. Oil-fried foods are unhealthier than air-fried foods. Air frying is thought to cut down on the calorie content in any meal by as much as 80% in some cases, and your food will be crispier because it's not absorbing oil. That is why air fryers are considered to be a good option for anyone who wants a fresher taste to their traditionally fried foods, e.g., French fries, without the 'soggy' and almost wet consistency that can sometimes come from frying in oil.

1.4 Different Air Fryers in The Market Today

When deciding which air fryer to buy, you need to know about the different types on the market. Overall, there are two main types, and the one you opt for needs to be a type that can fit comfortably on your kitchen countertop and do exactly what you need it to do. Everyone has different needs, so think about what you want to get out of your air fryer before splashing the cash. The two main air fryers on the modern market are:

- Basket air fryer, including a cylindrical basket air fryer
- Air fryer ovens

You may also hear about paddle air fryers. However, these are much less popular and aren't as widely available. Remember that regardless of which type of air fryer you opt for, you can still cook the same food quickly and with the same results. It's simply the pros and cons that make each one stands out. That's why it's essential to understand the fundamental differences. Let's look at each one in turn.

1.4.1 Basket Air Fryer

The basket air fryer is the most common type of air fryer you'll find on the market and there are many options which are quite low in price. Within this type of air fryer, you'll also see 'cylindrical basket air fryer'. This simply refers to where the heat comes from. In this case, the air is heated at the top of the fryer and then it circulates around your food, placed in the basket. Basket air fryers have, as the name suggests, a basket inside which is removable, and this is where you place your food to be cooked. However, as with any type of kitchen appliance, there are pros and cons.

Pros:
- Basket air fryers are widely available at good prices
- These types are quite compact and therefore need much less space on your countertop
- Ingredients are easy to add the basket and you can shake them to ensure even cooking
- Basket air fryers heat up quite quickly, sometimes in as little as 2 minutes
- These air fryers hold the air in and don't make your kitchen hot

Cons:
- Basket air fryers can be quite loud while they're cooking

- You cannot see the food while it is cooking, which means it may overcook if you don't set it properly
- Air flyers can only do one thing - cook food. There aren't as many features as possible with basket air fryers compared to oven air fryers
- Due to the compact size, basket air fryers only fit small dishes inside
- You will need to cook your food in batches if you have a large family, as basket air fryers have less capacity

1.4.2 Oven Air Fryers

The second option is an oven air fryer. This type of air fryer still cooks your food in the air, therefore ensuring crispy and fresh-tasting food, but rather than having baskets inside, these types have racks inside that hold baking trays. The air is created at the top of the oven and then blown downward to cook the food. However, these types of air fryers can do more than basket air fryers, i.e., they can toast, bake, broil and even rotisserie. Let's look at the pros and cons.

Pros:
- Several different cooking functions possible, as mentioned above
- Larger capacity. These are ideal for larger families and means you won't need to cook in batches
- The included glass door means you can see food as it is cooking
- Oven air fryers are quieter than basket air fryers
- Many different sizes of baking dishes can fit inside
- You can place your food higher or lower down in the oven, so you can control cooking time and intensity
- Depending upon the model, some parts of an oven air fryer are usually dishwasher safe

Cons:
- Larger size means oven air fryers aren't as compact and therefore take up more space on your countertop
- Oven air fryers are typically higher in cost because of the extra features on offer
- Unlike a basket air fryer, you can't shake your food mid-way
- Oven air fryers usually make your kitchen a little hotter than basket air fryers
- May take a longer time to preheat, compared to a basket air fryer

Within each type of air fryer, you will find different makes and models. Read reviews before making a purchasing choice and look closely at each type to decide which is going to suit your needs in the long-term. If you want your air fryer to complete many different cooking tasks, an oven air fryer is a better choice. However, if you don't need many features, perhaps a basket air fryer will be sufficient for you.

COLOR IMAGES:

In your air fryer culinary journey, accuracy is essential. This cookbook provides detailed recipes and, to enhance your cooking experience, we've also curated a high-definition digital collection of color photographs showcasing each dish. To keep the cookbook affordable, these photos are not included in the print version. Instead, they are available in a convenient PDF format, perfectly optimized for your smartphone or tablet. No need for email sign-up. Simply follow the link provided or scan the QR code below. This allows you to view, zoom in, and download these images for offline use, making your plant-based cooking both easier and more enjoyable. We hope this digital resource enriches your experience and helps you unlock the full potential of plant-based cuisine. Happy Cooking!

LINK: https://BookHip.com/LDXXPBZ

1.5 The Elements of an Air Fryer

Upon shopping for an air fryer, you'll quickly see the sheer number of makes and models on the market. However, as different as they appear, they all have essential parts. Understanding how those parts work in the cooking process helps you to get to know your new appliance better.

The three essential parts that all air fryers have include:
- Inner basket
- Outer basket (including the drawer)
- Cake pans
- Heating element

Of course, the outer part of every air fryer will be slightly different. More expensive models will be larger in capacity and will have more settings, compared to lower-cost models which tend to be smaller in capacity and have more basic functions.

Let's take a more detailed look at each of the elements that make up the whole air fryer.

Inner Basket

The inner basket is the part that holds your food and is therefore the main feature of any appliance. While your food is being cooked, it will sit side inside the basket and the air will circulate around it. Of course, that description leads you to believe that the basket will have holes around it, allowing the hot air to permeate through. Some models also feature baskets that have holes in the bottom, and this is designed to allow excess heat to leave the basket and, therefore, not overcook your food. You may also find some models that feature top vents intended to do the same thing. The holes in the inner basket also help excess fat to drip out of the bottom and into the bottom of the appliance, hence why it will need cleaning regularly. Of course, you're not adding oil to your food, as you're cooking in the air, but natural fats escape from certain ingredients and will need to drip away.

Outer Basket/drawer

The outer basket holds the inner basket, allowing your food to cook perfectly. This is also the part of the air fryer that catches the drips of fat or any crumbs of food that fall out of the inner basket during the cooking process. However, nothing will escape from the outer basket, as this part is fully encased, with no holes. The primary purpose of this outer basket is to allow ease of cleaning and to stop anything leaking onto your countertop. For your air fryer to turn on to cook your food, you will need to ensure that the outer basket is secured in place; most models simply won't switch on otherwise. It's effortless to remove and insert your outer basket as it fits snugly into the air fryer outer casing and will click in place. This part of the air fryer also has a drawer that sits underneath the main inner basket, and it is here where you will notice oil and grease collecting.

Cake Pan

Not all models have a cake pan included but you will find that many these days do. This is a part of the air fryer that is mostly used when baking, e.g., for cakes, as the name suggests. In that case, you will use this for cakes, breads, pizzas, and perhaps casseroles.

When using the cake pan, you won't use the inner basket. That is because when you're baking, you don't expect any food to drip out - however that does rely on you not overfilling your cake pan! Cake pans often have a non-stick lining so that whatever you make can slide out easily and many are made of stainless steel or aluminum. However, some modern models will feature silicone cake pans.

Heating Element

Without a doubt, the most important part of your air fryer is the heating element, something which all models need! The heating element turns the energy from the plug into heat, which then cooks your food without the need for oil. The electric cord and plug on your air fryer will need to be kept clean and most mode plug in a wind-around section on the back that allows you to store the cable and plug safely when your air fryer is not in use.

1.6 Tips & Tricks of Air Fryer Use

When learning how to use your air fryer, the first few attempts will be somewhat of a 'trial and error' kind of affair. This is completely normal with any new appliance. If you follow the guidelines on how to use your particular model, you will achieve your desired results very quickly after starting to use your air fryer. However, there are some common tricks and tips you can use that will allow you to master your new air fryer much faster and be able to start creating delicious meals and snacks from the get-go. Here we share some of the best tricks you can use.

- All makes and models vary across different brands, and it could be that your particular appliance has different temperature control settings to what you may be used to. It could be that your appliance doesn't have the exact temperature setting that you see written down in a recipe. If that's the case, the user manual should give you some advice on what temperature to go for.
- Many recipes will tell you to pre-heat your air fryer. While you can do this if you want to, it isn't necessary. Air fryers heat up extremely quickly and it will be at the desired temperature you have chosen within a few minutes at most.
- When using your air fryer, make sure that it is on a flat, even surface and allow around 5" space between the back of the fryer and any walls or other surfaces. This will allow the hot air to escape.
- When reading recipes, you may see that they call for specific dishes or cake tins. You don't necessarily have to go out buying many accessories for your new device. Some models will come with a few accessories included, but if you look in your kitchen cupboards, you may already have what you need. Most dishes and pans that are oven-safe can often be used in an air fryer - they simply need to be the right size to fit inside the basket.
- Some recipes will ask you to spray your food with a little oil. You might wonder what the point is if you're going to be air frying! However, some foods simply need a very small amount of sprayed oil to help them cook better. In that case, a small spray bottle is all you need to avoid going overboard.
- You can use a "sling" made of out aluminum foil to help you insert and remove accessories from your air fryer, e.g., cake tins. This makes the process much easier and avoids any potential for burns. While the air fryer is in use, you would simply tuck the edges of the foil sling inside and remove carefully once cooled.
- If you're cooking foods that are quite fatty, e.g., sausages, it's a good idea to add a small amount of water to the removable drawer underneath the inner basket. This will remove any smoke and will stop your food from becoming too hot.
- When cooking food, try and keep everything in one even layer if possible as this will make it easier to simply turn the food over at the halfway point and ensure even cooking.
- If you do need to use more than one layer of ingredients, be sure to give your basket a shake every so often, to ensure everything cooks evenly.
- Regardless of how many layers you use, never overcrowd the basket. You will not get the desired result and your food will be less than crispy. You may also find that certain parts of your food do not cook properly.
- To avoid any drips of fat from your food making its way onto your serving plate, make sure that you move the basket from the main drawer before serving your food.
- Parchment paper sprayed with a small amount of cooking oil can be placed in the bottom of the inner basket when cooking breaded items or anything with dough. This will prevent the food from sticking inside the basket holes or grooves.
- If you are cooking sandwiches in your air fryer, you can secure the top section of the bread with a toothpick. This will stop the air from dislodging the bread and affecting the outcome of your sandwich.

1.7 Common Troubleshooting Solutions

An air fryer is an electrical appliance and sometimes you may encounter a few issues that make you scratch your head and wonder how to overcome them. The good news is that issues are relatively common and therefore have solutions to them. Here are a few common issues many people encounter with air frying food and how to solve them.

If your food isn't that crispy …

Place less food inside your air fryer basket. The main issue here is overcrowding the basket, therefore not allowing the air to circulate freely and evenly during the cooking process. You should also make sure that you're not using too much sprayed oil if the recipe asks for it.

If you see white smoke

You might panic if you see white smoke making its way out of the air fryer, however this is quite a common sight. It is most likely because grease and oil from the food has dripped down into the drawer below the basket and is burning slightly. To prevent this, place a small amount of water in the drawer that sits underneath the basket.

If you see black smoke …

White smoke isn't a big issue when you're using an air fryer, but black smoke isn't the best sign. In this case, you need to switch off your appliance and look at the heating element. It's possible that some food has escaped onto the element and is burning on top of it. Allow everything to cool completely and clean thoroughly.

If your air fryer will not turn off …

Modern air fryers have a safety feature which often causes people to panic and think their appliance isn't turning off! There is often a delay when the appliance starts to shut down and once you have turned off the machine, you'll probably notice that the fan is still blowing air around. This shouldn't last for more than around 25 seconds at most. Simply wait and the machine should shut down on its own.

1.8 What Can't an Air Fryer Do?

As wonderful as an air fryer is, it does have its limitations. It isn't an appliance that can cook absolutely everything. However, you will find that as air fryers gain popularity, more and more recipes are being adapted to allow them to be cooked satisfactorily in this way. The following foods simply aren't suitable for air fryer or should never even be attempted.

- **Foods in a wet type of batter** - Breaded foods work very well in an air fryer, however a wet type of batter simply won't cook that well in an air fryer and will probably drip away into the bottom basket before it has any chance to cook.
- **Dense cake batters** - If you're attempting to make a cake in your air fryer, you'll find some great recipes. However, doughnuts or cakes that have a dense batter of flour, sour cream, and sugar, will not work so well. In this case, the air will simply dry the batter out, not giving you the fluffy and moist outcome, you desire. In this case, butter-based cake batters work better.
- **Excessively cheesy dishes** - Throughout this book you'll find recipes that contain cheese and for the most part, cheese works very well in your air fryer. However, if you're cooking an excessively cheesy dish, you're going to notice that most of it drips out into the bottom drawer and leaves you with little in the actual basket. You need to think about moderation when it comes to air fryers and cheese.
- **Whole chickens** - While very small whole chickens can be cooked inside an air fryer, medium or large whole chickens will not cook evenly. In that case, you will find some parts of the chicken will be overcooked and dry, while others only just cooked. Of course, there is also the potential for some parts to not cook properly at all, which is a health risk.
- **Bacon** - This one isn't necessarily a no, but it will leave you with a big mess to clean up. If you are going to cook bacon inside your air fryer, you'll need to line the basket with aluminum foil, to catch the grease. However, you will probably find that the natural fat from inside the bacon will spray out all over the sides and top of the fryer. If you have the time and patience to clean it, go ahead, but if not, it's probably best to avoid it.

- **Leafy greens** - The high speed of the air inside your air fryer is likely to make leafy greens move around too easily and as a result, they will cook very unevenly.

1.9 How to Clean an Air Fryer

Before you start cleaning your air fryer, you'll need to refer to the manual to get a thorough overview. All makes and models will need to be cleaned slightly differently and to avoid any possible breakages, it's best to read the manual carefully before use. However, there are some general cleaning guidelines you can follow to make sure that your air fryer is always clean. It's vital that you never use abrasive sponges or a brush with steel wire to clean the air fryer. This will simply scratch and damage the inside. Also, never be tempted to scratch away at any stuck food with a knife or anything metal. This will also damage the inside. Instead, allow the area to soak in warm, soapy water and it should release itself, making it much easier to clean. Of course, your air fryer is electrical so never submerge the whole thing in water and always make sure that you unplug it before you start to clean. The air fryer should be completely cool before you clean. After regular use, you may find that you notice an unpleasant smell coming from your appliance and if that's the case, it's likely that a small amount of food is stuck within one of the small corners or crevices. You can easily clean this with an old toothbrush. Old crumbs can easily accumulate in small areas and cause such smells over time, so a thorough clean occasionally will prevent this from happening. Be sure to clean your air fryer after every single use. This means you need to wash the basket, pan, and tray with warm, soapy water. However, some parts are suitable to be cleaned in a dishwasher - check your user manual to be sure before doing this. If you're cleaning manually, use a soft, damp cloth to clean the inside and use a small amount of regular dish soap to clean thoroughly. Then, dry with a dry, soft cloth and ensure all parts are totally dry before reassembling. You should also make sure that you wipe down the outside of your air fryer every so often and check the heating element occasionally to make sure oil residue isn't starting to build up. If so, a soft, damp cloth should allow you to remove build up. For a quick overview of a full clean after use, check out the steps below:

- Remove pans and baskets from your air fryer
- Wash with warm, soapy water, using a soft, non-abrasive sponge. At this point remove any grease or baked-on grime. You can soak these parts in warm, soapy water for up to 10 minutes
- Wipe the interior of the air fryer with a microfiber cloth and a small amount of dish soap. Once finished, use a clean, damp cloth to remove any soap residue
- Turn your air fryer upside down and wipe the heating element with a sponge or a damp cloth. Again, always use non-abrasive options here
- Wipe down the exterior of the air fryer with a damp cloth
- Ensure all parts are totally dry before putting the air fryer back together again.

1.10 Looking After Your Air Fryer

An air fryer is an electrical device and like all devices of this kind, it needs to be looked after to ensure it lasts longer. Air flyers are very easy to look after and maintain and you simply need to follow the instructions included with your appliance to ensure that it lasts the test of time. However, there are some general rules of thumb you can follow to keep your appliance ticking along nicely over the long-term.

- Always clean your air fryer after you've used it and follow the instructions included with your appliance to find out how to clean it. All air fryers need to be cleaned slightly differently
- Avoid using sponges or cloths that have rough or abrasive surfaces and edges. These can scratch the inside of your appliance and cause damage. A soft cloth is just as effective and will clean your air fryer adequately
- Completely submerging your air fryer in water is a huge no-no! This is an electrical appliance, and we all know that water and electricity do not make a very good pairing!
- After using your air fryer, unplug the device and allow it to cool completely before cleaning
- Do not use any parts of your air fryer in the dishwasher, unless your manufacturer instructions state that you can do so

- In some cases, you'll need to take your air fryer apart to a certain degree when cleaning. Follow instructions and do not put back together again until all parts are totally dry.

As you can see, a lot of looking after an air fryer is common sense but as long as you follow instructions, you can look forward to a long and happy air fryer lifespan. All that's left to do now is show you some truly delicious recipes you can start to make in your new gadget. Which one will you choose first.

I have added two annexes at the end of the book, where annex – A facilitates with shopping list for a week of diet and annex – B explains about the basic etiquette of washing and handling of food in the kitchen. Moreover, frequently asked questions along with measurement conversion charts are also added to improve cooking experiences.

1.11 Storage & Reheating

LEFTOVER FOOD	REFRIGERATION TIME	FREEZING TIME	SPECIAL INSTRUCTIONS
PASTA, RICE, AND GRAINS	3-5 days	3 months	Store in air-tight containers to avoid moisture build-up; may require reheating with a splash of water.
VEGATBLES	3-4 days	1-2 months	Blanch before freezing to preserve
FRUITS	5-7 days (if cut)	2-6 months	Can become soft; store without cutting for best quality.
SALADS	3-5 days	Not Recommended	Don't freeze due to wilting and high moisture content.
SEAFOOD	1-2 days	3-6 months	Pack tightly; risk of freezer burns
MEAT	3-4 days	2-6 months	Avoid freezer burn by sealing tightly; flavor may diminish over extended time.
DAIRY ITEMS	1-2 days	1-2 months	Can experience separation or curdling; best used in cooked dishes after freezing.
SMOOTHIES	1-2 days	4-6 months	Store fruits and other ingredients in zip-lock bags to avoid moisture and items getting rotten
BAKED ITEMS	3-7 days	2-3 months	Allow to cool completely before freezing; frosting or fillings may change in texture.
SOUPS AND STEWS	3-4 days	4-6 months	Cool before freezing; might require mixing after thawing due to possible separation.

*NOTE: Best tip to store food items is to divide your meals into smaller portion sizes that can be consumed at a single time. Place each portion in an airtight zip-lock bag. This tip might help support better freezing to avoid repeated reheating and save the nutritional content of foods.

2 QUICK & EASY RECIPES

2.1 French Toast

Preparation Time: 5 mins |
Cooking Time: 10 mins | Serving 1

Ingredients:

- Egg - 1
- Bread – 2 slices
- Milk – ½ cup (30 ml)
- Flour – 2 tbsp (30 g)
- Caster sugar – 3 tbsp (45 g)
- Cinnamon – 1 tsp (5 g)
- Vanilla extract – ½ tsp (2.5 g)

Method:

1. Preheat your air fryer to 193°C (380°F)
2. Cut your bread into three pieces
3. Combine all your ingredients in a bowl
4. Cover the bread with the mixture
5. Take a piece of parchment paper and lay it inside the air fryer
6. Arrange the bread on the parchment paper
7. Cook for 5 minutes on each side

Nutritional Facts

Calories – 332 | Fat - 3g | Carbs - 24g | Protein - 6g | Sugar – 2g | Fiber – 2g | Potassium - 134mg | Sodium – 220mg | Cholesterol – 180mg

2.2 Air Fryer Eggs

Preparation Time: 5 mins |
Cooking Time: 15 mins | Serving 1

Ingredients:

- Eggs - 4
- Cheese – 4 oz (114 g)
- Salt and Pepper – To taste
- Greased ramekin dishes - 2

Method:

1. Crack two eggs into one dish
2. Add some cheese to each dish
3. Season to your liking
4. Place in the air fryer and cook for 15 minutes at 180°C (350°F) for 15 minutes

Nutrition per serving:

Calories – 300 | Fat - 2g | Carbs - 15g | Protein - 5g | Sugar – 1g | Fiber – 0g | Potassium - 13mg | Sodium – 380mg | Cholesterol – 425mg

2.3 Easy Pancakes

Preparation Time - 5 mins |
Cooking Time - 8 mins | Serves 1

Ingredients:

- Eggs - 3
- Plain flour – 4 oz (114 g)
- Milk – ½ cup (118 ml)
- Apple sauce – 2 tbsp (30 ml)
- Greased ramekin dishes - 5

Method:

1. Preheat your air fryer to 150°C (300°F)
2. Blend all your ingredients until smooth
3. Transfer the batter into the ramekin dishes
4. Fry for 8 minutes
5. Serve with any topping you desire

Nutrition per serving:

Calories – 250 | Fat - 2g | Carbs - 20g | Protein - 4g | Sugar – 2g | Fiber – 1g | Potassium - 45mg | Sodium – 170mg | Cholesterol – 255mg

2.4 Morning Wraps

Preparation Time: 5 mins |
Cooking Time: 6 mins | Serving: 1

Ingredients:

- Corn tortillas – 2 crushed
- Eggs - 2
- Flour tortillas - 2
- Jalapeño pepper – 1(slices)
- Avocado – 1 thinly sliced
- Ranchero sauce – 4 tbsp (60 ml)
- Pinto beans – 0.8 oz (22 g) (cooked)

Method:

1. Add the eggs, jalapeño, sauce, the corn tortillas, the avocado, and the pinto beans to the flour tortillas
2. Fold up your wrap and put inside the air fryer
3. Cook at 150°C (300°F) for 6 minutes

Nutrition per serving:

Calories – 450 | Fat - 3g | Carbs - 21g | Protein - 7g | Sugar – 3g | Fiber – 5g | Potassium - 50mg | Sodium – 470mg | Cholesterol – 190mg

2.5 Cheese & Ham in Puff Pastry

Preparation Time: 5 mins |
Cooking Time: 14 mins | Serving: 1

Ingredients:

- Eggs - 4
- Puff pastry – 1 piece
- Cheddar cheese - 4 tbsp (60 ml) (grated)
- Ham – 4 slices

Method:

1. Cut your pastry into four equal pieces
2. Cook two pieces of the pastry inside the air fryer for 8 minutes at 200°C (390°F)
3. Make a hole in the middle of the cooked pastry
4. Add some cheese and ham into the middle, along with one egg
5. Cook for another 6 minutes
6. Repeat the process with your remaining ingredients

Nutrition per serving:

Calories – 450 | Fat - 5g | Carbs - 21g | Protein - 8g | Sugar – 2g | Fiber – 1g | Potassium - 65mg | Sodium – 400mg | Cholesterol – 280mg

2.6 Spanish Frittata

Preparation Time: 5 mins |
Cooking Time: 5 mins | Serving: 1

Ingredients:

- Olive oil – 1 tbsp (15 ml)
- Eggs - 3
- Chorizo sausage – 1 (sliced)
- Potato – 1 (boiled)
- Feta cheese – 1.7 oz (48 g) (crumbled)
- Sweetcorn – 1.7 oz (48 g)
- Salt – For seasoning

Method:

1. Coat your frying basket in oil and add the chorizo, potato, and corn
2. Cook at 180°C (350°F) until the sausage has browned
3. Beat together the eggs with the salt and transfer to the pan
4. Add the feta and cook for 5 minutes

Nutrition per serving:

Calories – 460 | Fat - 4g | Carbs - 30g | Protein - 8g | Sugar – 2g | Fiber – 3g | Potassium - 45mg | Sodium – 520mg | Cholesterol – 225mg

2.7 Ham & Egg Bites

Preparation Time: 5 mins |
Cooking Time: 15 mins | Serving: 1

Ingredients:

- Bread – 8 slices
- Eggs – 4 large
- Ham – 2 slices
- Salt and pepper – To taste
- Greased ramekin dishes - 4

Method:

1. Roll out each piece of toast with a rolling pan
2. Place inside the ramekin dishes
3. Add ham around the bread
4. Crack one egg into each dish and season
5. Cook at 150°C (300°F) for 15 minutes

Nutrition per serving:

Calories – 450 | Fat - 2g | Carbs - 28g | Protein - 8g | Sugar – 4g | Fiber – 3g | Potassium - 67mg | Sodium – 350mg | Cholesterol – 185mg

2.8 Vegetable Hash Browns

Preparation Time: 30 mins |
Cooking Time: 20 mins | Serving: 1

Ingredients:

- Olive oil – 2 tbsp
- Potatoes - 4 grated
- Chopped onion - 1
- Red pepper – 1 chopped
- Green pepper – 1 chopped
- Bicarbonate of soda – 2 tbsp (30 g)
- Cayenne pepper – 1tsp (5 g)
- Salt and pepper – To taste

Method:

1. Place the potatoes in a large bowl of water with the bicarbonate of soda. Leave to soak for 30 minutes
2. Pat the potatoes dry and place into a bowl
3. Add the spices and oil, combining everything well
4. Cook for 10 minutes at 180°C (350°F)
5. Add the other vegetables and cook for another 10 minutes

Nutrition per serving:

Calories – 400 | Fat - 5g | Carbs - 21g | Protein - 7g | Sugar – 3g | Fiber – 5g | Potassium - 35mg | Sodium – 450mg | Cholesterol – 0mg

2.9 Air Fryer Omelet

Preparation Time: 5 mins |
Cooking Time: 12 mins | Serving: 1

Ingredients:

- Eggs - 2
- Milk – ¼ cup (59 ml)
- Cheese – 4 oz (114 g) (grated)
- Salt – To taste

Method:

1. Combine the eggs and milk with a little salt
2. Grease a medium cooking pan and transfer the mixture inside
3. Place the pan inside the fryer and cook for 10 minutes at 150°C (300°F)
4. Add the cheese just before the omelet has finished and cook for another 2 minutes.

Nutrition per serving:

Calories – 280 | Fat - 5g | Carbs - 29g | Protein - 8g | Sugar – 3g | Fiber – 0g | Potassium - 30mg | Sodium – 600mg | Cholesterol – 380mg

2.10 Full & Healthy Peppers

Preparation Time: 5 mins |
Cooking Time: 10 mins | Serving: 1

Ingredients:

- Olive oil – 2 tbsp (30 ml)
- Eggs - 4
- Bell pepper – 1 (cut into slices)
- Salt and pepper - To taste

Method:

1. Rub the oil over the peppers and crack one egg into each
2. Arrange the peppers inside the air fryer basket and cook for 13 minutes at 180°C (350°F)
3. Season before serving

Nutrition per serving:

Calories – 450 | Fat - 2g | Carbs - 21g | Protein - 7g | Sugar – 3g | Fiber – 2g | Potassium - 50mg | Sodium – 370mg | Cholesterol – 720mg

2.11 Sausage Surprise

Preparation Time: 5 mins | Cooking Time: 3 mins | Serving: 1

Ingredients:

- Sausages – 8 chopped
- Cheese – 2 slices chopped
- Pizza dough – 1 piece

Method:

1. Roll the pizza dough out and cut into two pieces
2. Add a little sausage and then a little cheese to the dough
3. Roll and create a triangle shape
4. Cook for 3 minutes at 190°C (370°F)
5. Repeat with another piece of dough.

Nutrition per serving:

Calories – 470 | Fat - 9g | Carbs - 35g | Protein - 10g | Sugar – 3.5g | Fiber – 1.5g | Potassium - 65mg | Sodium – 750mg | Cholesterol – 40mg

2.12 Cheesy Toast

Preparation Time: 5 mins | Cooking Time: 7 mins | Serving: 1

Ingredients:

- Melted butter – 1tbsp
- Bread – 4 slices
- Cheese – 2 slices
- Cooked bacon – 5 slices

Method:

1. Spread the butter onto the bread and place in the air fryer
2. Add the cheese and bacon
3. Add the other slice of bread on top
4. Cook for 4 minutes at 180°C (350°F)
5. Turn the toast over and cook for a further 3 minutes

Nutrition per serving:

Calories – 450 | Fat - 4g | Carbs - 21g | Protein - 5g | Sugar – 3g | Fiber – 1g | Potassium - 70mg | Sodium – 650mg | Cholesterol – 30mg

2.13 Breakfast Sandwich

Preparation Time: 5 mins |
Cooking Time: 18 mins | Serving: 1

Ingredients:

- Egg – 1
- Butter – 2 tbsp (30 g)
- Sandwich bread – 2 slices
- Vanilla extract – ¼ tsp (1 ml)
- Cheese – 4 slices
- Ham – 4 slices
- Turkey – 4 slices

Method:

1. Combine the egg and vanilla
2. Make a sandwich with the bread, cheese, meats and top with the other slice of bread
3. Coat the sandwich in butter and dip in the egg mixture
4. Cook for 10 minutes at 200°C (390°F)
5. Turnover and cook for a further 8 minutes.

Nutrition per serving:

Calories – 300 | Fat - 7g | Carbs - 22g | Protein - 6g | Sugar – 3g | Fiber – 2g | Potassium - 120mg | Sodium – 450mg | Cholesterol – 180mg

2.14 Quick Morning Doughnuts

Preparation Time: 5 mins |
Cooking Time: 5 mins | Serving: 4

Ingredients:

- Pizza-style dough – 1 packet
- Butter – 1 tbsp (15 ml)
- Jam – 5 tbsp (75 g)
- Sugar – 5tbsp (75 g)

Method:

1. Cook the dough in the air fryer for 5 minutes at 200°C (390°F)
2. Dip the cooked doughnuts in the sugar and coat completely
3. Pipe the jam inside the doughnuts

Nutrition per serving:

Calories – 332 | Fat - 3g | Carbs - 24g | Protein - 6g | Sugar – 6g | Fiber – 1.2g | Potassium - 150mg | Sodium – 300mg | Cholesterol – 15mg

2.15 Spinach & Eggs

Preparation Time: 5 mins |
Cooking Time: 20 mins | Serving: 2

Ingredients:

- Olive oil – 1 tbsp (15 ml)
- Spinach – 17 oz (481 g)
- Deli ham – 7 oz (198g) (sliced)
- Milk - 2 tbsp (30 ml)
- Eggs - 4
- Salt and pepper – To taste
- Ramekin dishes - 4

Method:

1. Preheat the air fryer to 170°C (350°F)
2. Add the wilted spinach, ham, a quarter of the milk, and 1 egg into each dish and season
3. Cook for 20 minutes
4. Cool before consumption

Nutrition per serving:

Calories – 350 | Fat – 3g | Carbs - 21g | Protein - 8g | Sugar – 9g | Fiber – 4g | Potassium - 800mg | Sodium – 550mg | Cholesterol – 190mg

2.16 Breakfast Pockets

Preparation Time: 5 mins |
Cooking Time: 10 mins | Serving: 2

Ingredients:

- Eggs - 5
- Puff pastry - 1
- Sausages – 4 (cooked)
- Bacon – 1.7 oz (48 g) (cooked)
- Cheese – 1.7 oz (48 g) (grated)

Method:

1. Scramble your eggs in a pan and halfway through, add the bacon and sausage
2. Cut your paste into rectangles
3. Add some of the mixture to half the pastry and fold over
4. Seal the edges with a fork and cook in your air fryer for 10 minutes at 180°C (350°F)

Nutrition per serving:

Calories – 500 | Fat - 2g | Carbs - 14g | Protein - 7g | Sugar – 2g | Fiber – 0.7g | Potassium - 100mg | Sodium – 620mg | Cholesterol – 255mg

2.17 Easy Boiled Eggs

Preparation Time: 2 mins |

Cooking Time: 15 mins | Serving: 1

Ingredients:

- Eggs - 4
- Cayenne pepper – 1 tsp (5 g)
- Salt and pepper – To taste

Method:

1. Preheat the air fryer to 220°C (400°F)
2. Place the eggs inside the fryer and cook for 15 minutes at 200°C (390°F)
3. Place the eggs in ice cold water and leave to cool for 5 minutes
4. Cut the eggs and season with the spices

Nutrition per serving:

Calories – 400 | Fat - 2g | Carbs - 21g | Protein - 8g | Sugar – 3g | Fiber – 0g | Potassium - 35mg | Sodium – 140mg | Cholesterol – 744mg

2.18 Paprika Hash

Preparation Time: 5 mins |

Cooking Time: 20 mins | Serving: 2

Ingredients:

- Olive oil – 2 tbsp (30 ml)
- Bacon – 2 slices (chopped)
- Potatoes - 2 (cubed)
- Smoked paprika – 1 tbsp (15 g)
- Salt and pepper – To taste

Method:

1. Preheat your air fryer to 200°C (390°F)
2. Combine the oil, potatoes, bacon, and seasonings
3. Place in the fryer and cook for 16 minutes, stirring regularly

Nutrition per serving:

Calories – 650 | Fat - 2g | Carbs - 28g | Protein - 8g | Sugar – 4g | Fiber – 2.5g | Potassium - 500mg | Sodium – 580mg | Cholesterol – 25mg

2.19 Egg "Sandwiches"

Preparation Time: 5 mins |

Cooking Time: 7 mins | Serving: 2

Ingredients:

- Salt and pepper – To taste
- Eggs - 2
- Bread – 2 (slices)

Method:

1. Create a hole in the middle of your bread and crack an egg into each one
2. Season and place in the air fryer, cooking for 5 minutes at 180°C (350°F)
3. Turnover and cook for another 2 minutes
4. Repeat with the other slice of bread

Nutrition per serving:

Calories – 332 | Fat - 3g | Carbs - 24g | Protein - 6g | Sugar – 10g | Fiber – 2g | Potassium - 200mg | Sodium – 400mg | Cholesterol – 164mg

2.20 Creamy Breakfast Treats

Preparation Time: 7 mins |

Cooking Time: 5 mins | Serving: 2

Ingredients:

- Egg – 1 (medium)
- Milk – 1 tbsp (15 ml)
- Bread – 2 (slices)
- Cream cheese – 1 tbsp (15 g) (soft)
- Jam – 1 tbsp (15 g)

Method:

1. Take one slice of the bread and add some jam into the middle
2. Take the other slice and add the cream cheese
3. Spread both across the edges
4. Whisk the eggs and the milk together
5. Set your fryer to 190°C (370°F)
6. Dip your sandwich into the egg and place in the fryer basket
7. Cook for 5 minutes, turn, and cook for another 2 minutes

Nutrition per serving:

Calories – 450 | Fat - 3g | Carbs - 20g | Protein - 8g | Sugar – 3g | Fiber – 1g | Potassium - 350mg | Sodium – 300mg | Cholesterol – 107mg

3 FISH & SEAFOOD RECIPES

3.1 Shrimp Pops

Preparation Time: 5 mins |

Cooking Time: 6 mins | Serving: 2

Ingredients:
- Shrimp pieces – 10 oz (284 g) (popcorn shrimp will work well)
- Cayenne pepper – 1 tsp (5 g)
- Salt and pepper – To taste

Method:
1. Place the shrimp inside the air fryer and cook for 6 minutes at 190°C (370°F)
2. Shake after 3 minutes
3. Season to your liking before serving

Nutrition per serving:

Calories – 332 | Fat - 3g | Carbs - 24g | Protein - 6g | Sugar – 10g | Fiber – 0.5g | Potassium - 250mg | Sodium – 480mg | Cholesterol – 172mg

3.2 Crab Stuffed Mushrooms

Preparation Time: 5 mins |

Cooking Time: 18 mins | Serving: 2

Ingredients:
- Crab – 10 oz (284 g)
- Egg - 1
- Mushrooms – 17 oz (481 g)
- Red onion – ½ (chopped)
- Celery sticks – 2 (diced)
- Breadcrumbs – 1.2 oz (34 g) (seasoned)
- Cheese – 1.7 oz (48 g) (grated)
- Oregano – 1 tsp (5 g)
- Hot sauce – 1 tsp (5 ml)

Method:
1. Preheat your air fryer to 190°C (370°F)
2. Place a piece of parchment inside your air fryer and spray with a small amount of cooking oil
3. Arrange the mushrooms with the tops facing down
4. Combine onions, celery, breadcrumbs, egg, crab, most of the cheese, oregano, and hot sauce
5. Place the mixture inside the mushrooms and sprinkle the rest of the cheese on top
6. Cook for 18 minutes

Nutrition per serving:

Calories – 500 | Fat - 5g | Carbs - 21g | Protein - 8g | Sugar – 2g | Fiber – 2.8g | Potassium - 260mg | Sodium – 470mg | Cholesterol – 95mg

3.3 Zingy Shrimp

Preparation Time: 5 mins |

Cooking Time: 8 mins | Serving: 2

Ingredients:
- Olive oil – 1 tbsp (15 ml)
- Shrimp – 10 oz (284 g)
- Lemon – 1 (juice)
- Garlic powder – 0.25 tsp (1.2 g)
- Paprika – 0.25 tsp (1.2 g)
- Lemon – 1 (sliced)
- Pepper – 1 tsp (5 g)

Method:
1. Heat your air fryer to 200°C (390°F)
2. Combine the lemon juice, pepper, garlic powder, paprika, and the olive oil
3. Coat the shrimp with the mixture and place in the air fryer
4. Cook for 8 minutes

Nutrition per serving:

Calories – 400 | Fat - 19g | Carbs - 24g | Protein - 6g | Sugar – 3g | Fiber – 0.7g | Potassium - 250mg | Sodium – 315mg | Cholesterol – 180mg

3.4 Easy Bread crumbed Fish

Preparation Time: 5 mins |

Cooking Time: 12 mins | Serving: 2

Ingredients:
- Olive oil – 4 tbsp (60 ml)
- Egg – 1 (beaten)
- Breadcrumbs – 7 oz (198 g)
- Fish – 4 (fillets)

Method:
1. Heat your air fryer to 160°C (320°F)
2. Combine the olive oil and the breadcrumbs
3. Dip the fish in the egg, breadcrumbs, and place inside the air fryer
4. Cook for 12 minutes

Nutrition per serving:

Calories – 600 | Fat - 20g | Carbs - 22g | Protein - 8g | Sugar – 3g | Fiber – 1.2g | Potassium - 280mg | Sodium – 360mg | Cholesterol – 60mg

3.5 Asian Fish Patties

Preparation Time: 5 mins |

Cooking Time: 8 mins | Serving: 2

Ingredients:
- Breadcrumbs – 1 oz (28 g)
- Salmon – 1 can (drained)
- Eggs - 2
- Salt – ¼ tsp (1 g)
- Thai red curry – 1.5 tbsp (22.5 g) (paste)
- Brown sugar – 1.5 tbsp (22.5 g)
- Lime – 1 (zest)

Method:
1. Combine all ingredients together
2. Create patties that are around 1" thick
3. Cook the patties in the air fryer at 160°C (320°F) for 4 minutes on each side

Nutrition per serving:

Calories – 553 | Fat - 3g | Carbs - 29g | Protein - 6g | Sugar – 1g | Fiber – 0.9g | Potassium - 380mg | Sodium – 390mg | Cholesterol – 90mg

3.6 Simple Fish Fingers

Preparation Time: 5 mins |

Cooking Time: 8 mins | Serving: 1

Ingredients:
- Dressing:
1. Salt and pepper – To taste
2. Mixed herbs – 1 tsp (5 g)
3. Thyme – 1 tsp (5 g)
- Parsley – 1 tsp (5 g)
- Small lemon – 1 (juice)
- Fish – 1 (fillet)
- Flour – 1.7 oz (48 g)
- Egg – 1 (beaten)
- Bread – 2 Slices (grated and seasoned)

Method:
1. Preheat your air fryer to 160°C (320°F)
2. Combine the fish, seasonings, lemon juice and mixed herbs in a blender
3. Create finger shapes out of the mixture
4. First dip in the flour, then the egg, and finally the breadcrumbs
5. Cook for 8 minutes

Nutrition per serving:

Calories – 655 | Fat - 12g | Carbs - 30g | Protein - 6g | Sugar – 1g | Fiber – 1.5g | Potassium - 390mg | Sodium – 415mg | Cholesterol – 65mg

3.7 Salmon Burgers

Preparation Time: 5 mins |

Cooking Time: 10 mins | Serving: 2

Ingredients:
- Egg - 1
- Salmon – 14 oz (396 g)
- Onion – 1 (diced)
- Breadcrumbs – 7 oz (198 g)
- Dill weed – 1 tsp (5 g)

Method:
1. Combine the egg, onion, dill weed, salmon and breadcrumbs
2. Create burger shapes and place into the air fryer
3. Cook for 5 minutes at 150°C (300°F)
4. Turn and cook for another 5 minutes

Nutrition per serving:

Calories – 590 | Fat - 10g | Carbs - 31g | Protein - 6g | Sugar – 2g | Fiber – 1.8g | Potassium - 360mg | Sodium – 310mg | Cholesterol – 85mg

3.8 Spicy Shrimp Boil

Preparation Time: 5 mins |

Cooking Time: 12 mins | Serving: 2

Ingredients:
- Shrimp – 10 oz (284 g) (cooked)
- Sausage – 14 pieces
- Parboiled potatoes – 5 (halved)
- Small corn – 4 (pieces)
- Onion – 1 (diced)
- Old bay – 3 tbsp (45 g) (seasoning)

Method:
1. Combine all ingredients
2. Line the air fryer with foil
3. Cook at 200°C (390°F) for 6 minutes
4. Stir and cook for another 6 minutes.

Nutrition per serving:

Calories – 450 | Fat - 9g | Carbs - 21g | Protein - 6g | Sugar – 1g | Fiber – 3.5g | Potassium - 360mg | Sodium – 800mg | Cholesterol – 95mg

3.9 Fish Taco Bowls

Preparation Time: 5 mins |

Cooking Time: 12 mins | Serving: 2

Ingredients:
- Fish – 14 oz (396 g) (pieces)
- Cauliflower rice – 10 oz (284 g)
- Avocado – 1 (sliced)
- Chili powder – 1 tsp (5 g)
- Paprika – ½ tsp (2.5 g)
- Red onions – 0.8 oz (22 g) (pickled)
- Sour cream – 0.8 oz (22 g)
- Cumin – ½ tsp (2.5 g)
- Lime juice – 1 tbsp (15 ml)
- Fresh coriander – 0.8 oz (22 g)
- Sriracha – 1 tbsp (15 ml)

Method:
1. Season the fish with the spices
2. Cook the fish in the air fryer at 200°C (390°F) for about 12 minutes
3. Meanwhile, cook the cauliflower rice according to instructions and add the coriander and lime juice once cooked
4. Divide the mixture between your serving bowls along with the fish, red onions, and avocado
5. Drizzle the sriracha and sour cream on top

Nutrition per serving:

Calories – 600 | Fat - 23g | Carbs - 24g | Protein - 6g | Sugar – 3g | Fiber – 6.8g | Potassium - 380mg | Sodium – 420mg | Cholesterol – 60mg

3.10 Air Fryer Scallops

Preparation Time: 5 mins |

Cooking Time: 4 mins | Serving: 2

Ingredients:
- Pepper and salt – To taste (dressings)
- Olive oil – 1 tbsp (15 ml)
- Scallops - 6

Method:
1. Brush the fillets with olive oil and season
2. Place in the air fryer and cook at 200°C (390°F) for 2 mins
3. Turn and cook for another 2 minutes

Nutrition per serving:

Calories – 500 | Fat - 9g | Carbs - 21g | Protein - 7g | Sugar – 2g | Fiber – 0.6g | Potassium - 380mg | Sodium – 320mg | Cholesterol – 40mg

3.11 Air Fryer Mussels

Preparation Time: 5 mins |

Cooking Time: 5 mins | Serving: 2

Ingredients:
- Butter – 1 tbsp (15 ml)
- Mussels – 14 oz (396 g) (cleaned and soaked)
- Water – 0.8 cups (189 ml)
- Basil – 1 Tbsp (15 g)
- Parsley – 1 tsp (5 g)
- Garlic – 2 tsp (10 g) (minced)
- Chives – 1 tsp (5 g)

Method:
1. Place all ingredients inside the air fryer and set to 180°C (350°F)
2. Cook for 3 minutes
3. If the mussels haven't opened, cook for a further 2 minutes

Nutrition per serving:
Calories – 332 | Fat - 3g | Carbs - 24g | Protein - 6g | Sugar – 10g | Fiber – 1.6g | Potassium - 260mg | Sodium – 280mg | Cholesterol – 45mg

3.12 Boozy Fish Tacos

Preparation Time: 5 mins |

Cooking Time: 15 mins | Serving: 1

Ingredients:
- Dressings:
- Salt and pepper – To taste
- Cumin – 1 Tbsp (15 g)
- Chili powder – ½ tsp (2.5 g)
- Corn tortillas – 2 (soft)
- Flour – 10 oz (284 g) (plain)
- Cornstarch – 10 oz (284 g)
- Beer – 1 can
- Eggs - 2

Method:
1. Combine the eggs and beer
2. Separately, combine the cornstarch, chili powder, flour, cumin, and salt and pepper
3. Dip the fish in the egg mixture then the flour mixture
4. Set your fryer to 180°C (350°F) and cook for 15 minutes
5. Serve in the tortillas

Nutrition per serving:
Calories – 332 | Fat - 3g | Carbs - 24g | Protein - 6g | Sugar – 10g | Fiber – 1.8g | Potassium - 270mg | Sodium – 390mg | Cholesterol – 185mg

3.13 Herby Tilapia

Preparation Time: 5 mins |

Cooking Time: 10 mins | Serving: 1

Ingredients:
- Dressings:
4. Salt and pepper – To taste
5. Olive oil – 2 tsp (10 ml)
6. Fresh parsley – 2 tsp (10 g) (chopped)
7. Fresh chives – 2 tsp (10 g) (chopped)
8. Garlic – 1 tsp (5 g) (minced)
- Tilapia fillets

Method:
1. Preheat your air fryer to 200°C (390°F)
2. Combine the olive oil with the chives, garlic, parsley, and seasoning
3. Coat the fish fillets
4. Place the fish into the air fryer and cook for 10 minutes

Nutrition per serving:

Calories – 650 | Fat - 19g | Carbs - 24g | Protein - 9g | Sugar – 2g | Fiber – 0.5g | Potassium - 260mg | Sodium – 210mg | Cholesterol – 60mg

3.14 Tartar Battered Fish Sticks

Preparation Time: 5 mins |

Cooking Time: 12 mins | Serving: 2

Ingredients:
- Cod fillets – 14 oz (396 g) (sliced)
- Mayonnaise – 6 tbsp (90 g)
- Dill pickle – 2 tbsp (30 g)
- Seafood – 1 tsp (seasoning)
- Breadcrumbs – 10.5 oz (284 g)

Method:
1. Preheat the air fryer to 200°C (390°F)
2. Combine the mayonnaise, seafood seasoning, and dill pickle
3. Add the fish and coat
4. Dip the fish in the breadcrumbs and place in the air fryer
5. Cook for 12 minutes

Nutrition per serving:

Calories – 690 | Fat - 19g | Carbs - 31g | Protein - 13g | Sugar – 3g | Fiber – 1.0g | Potassium - 300mg | Sodium – 360mg | Cholesterol – 50mg

3.15 Coconut Shrimp

Preparation Time: 5 mins |

Cooking Time: 8 mins | Serving: 2

Ingredients:
- Raw shrimp – 10.5 oz (284 g)
- Flour – 8 oz (224 g)
- Honey – 4 tbsp (60 ml)
- Eggs - 2
- Coconut – 5 oz (142 g) (flaked)
- Serrano chili – 1 (sliced)
- Breadcrumbs – 0.8 oz (189 g)
- Lime juice – 0.2 cups (47 ml)
- Salt and pepper – To taste

Method:
1. Combine the flour and pepper
2. Separately, beat the eggs
3. In another bowl mix breadcrumbs and coconut
4. Dip each of the shrimp in the flour mix then the egg and then cover in the breadcrumbs
5. Place in the air fryer and cook at 200°C (390°F) for 6-8 mins
6. Turn halfway through
7. Combine the honey, lime juice, and chili to serve

Nutrition per serving:
Calories – 630 | Fat - 19g | Carbs - 30g | Protein - 13g | Sugar – 2g | Fiber – 4g | Potassium - 360mg | Sodium – 310mg | Cholesterol – 165mg

4 VEGETARIAN PLATE RECIPES

4.1 Aubergine Parmesan

Preparation Time: 10 mins |

Cooking Time: 12 mins | Serving: 2

Ingredients:
- Dressings:
    - Salt and pepper – To taste
    - Italian seasoning – 1 tsp (seasonings)
- Whole wheat flour – 3 tbsp (45 g)
- Parmesan cheese – 3 tbsp (45 g) (grated)
- Egg - 1
- Aubergine – 1 (halved)
- Bread – 4 slices (grated)
- Water – 1 tbsp (15 ml)
- Marinara sauce – 5 tbsp (75 ml)
- Cheese – 1 oz (28 g) (grated)

Method:
1. Add a little salt to both sides of the aubergine
2. Combine the egg, flour, and water
3. Take a plate and add the breadcrumbs, parmesan, and Italian seasoning, combining well
4. Dip the aubergine into the egg mixture and the breadcrumbs
5. Preheat the air fryer to 200°C (390°F) and place the aubergine inside
6. Cook for 8 minutes
7. Add the marinara sauce and mozzarella on top and cook for another 2 minutes

Nutrition per serving:

Calories – 690 | Fat - 19g | Carbs - 31g | Protein - 13g | Sugar – 3g | Fiber – 7g | Potassium - 230mg | Sodium – 430mg | Cholesterol – 55mg

4.2 Citrus Cauliflower

Preparation Time: 5 mins |

Cooking Time: 18 mins | Serving: 2

Ingredients:
- Cauliflower – 1 (separated into florets)
- Olive oil – 2 tsp (10 ml)
- Water – 0.8 cups (189 ml)
- Flour – 7 oz (198 g) (plain)
- Garlic cloves – 2 (minced)
- Ginger – 1 tsp (5 g) (minced)
- Orange juice – 0.6 cups (141 ml)
- White vinegar – 3 tbsp (45 ml)
- Red pepper – ½ tsp (2.5 g) (flakes)
- Sesame oil – 1 tsp (5 ml)
- Brown sugar – 3.5 oz (99 g)
- Soy sauce – 3 tbsp (45 ml)
- Cornstarch – 1 tbsp (15 g)
- Salt and pepper – To taste

Method:
1. Combine the water, salt, and flour
2. Dip each floret of cauliflower into the mixture
3. Arrange in the air fryer and cook for 15 minutes at 200°C (390°F)
4. Combine the rest of the ingredients in a saucepan and bring to a simmer for 3 minutes
5. Drizzle the sauce over the cauliflower

Nutrition per serving:

Calories – 550 | Fat - 21g | Carbs - 30g | Protein - 13g | Sugar – 1g | Fiber – 6g | Potassium - 250mg | Sodium – 620mg | Cholesterol – 0mg

4.3 Cheese Tikka

Preparation Time: 2 hours |

Cooking Time: 6 mins | Serving: 2

Ingredients:
- Skewers – 8 (metal)
- Onion – 1 (chopped)
- Yellow pepper – 1 (chopped)
- Red pepper – 1 (chopped)
- Green pepper – 1 (chopped)
- Chopped coriander – 2 tbsp (30 g)
- Lemon – 1 (juice)
- Fenugreek leaves – 1 tbsp (15 g) (dried)
- Turmeric powder – 1 tsp (5 g)
- Gram masala – 1 tsp (5 g)
- Red chili powder – 1 tsp (5 g)
- Ginger garlic – 1 tsp (5 g) (paste)
- Yogurt – 0.8 cups (189 g)
- Olive oil – 1 tbsp (15 ml)
- Paneer cheese – 8.8 oz (250 g) (cubed)

Method:
1. Combine the yogurt, garlic paste, red chili powder, gram masala, turmeric powder, lemon juice, fenugreek, and chopped coriander
2. Add the cheese and coat well. Leave in the refrigerator for 2 hours
3. Take your skewers and add the cheese, peppers, and onions alternately
4. Add a little oil and place in the air fryer
5. Cook for 3 minutes at 200°C (390°F)
6. Turn and cook for 3 more minutes

Nutrition per serving:

Calories – 690 | Fat - 19g | Carbs - 31g | Protein - 13g | Sugar – 3g | Fiber – 6g | Potassium - 280mg | Sodium – 320mg | Cholesterol – 60mg

4.4 Air Fryer Ravioli

Preparation Time: 5 mins |

Cooking Time: 12 mins | Serving: 2

Ingredients:
- Ravioli – 1 pack
- Olive oil – 1 tbsp (15 ml)
- Buttermilk – 0.8 cups (189 ml)
- Breadcrumbs – 7 oz (198 g)
- Marinara sauce – 5 tbsp (75 ml)

Method:
1. Preheat the air fryer to 200°C (390°F)
2. Place the buttermilk in a bowl and place the breadcrumbs in another bowl
3. Dip each piece of ravioli in the buttermilk and then the breadcrumbs
4. Place in the air fryer and cook for 7 minutes
5. Add some oil if the ravioli becomes dry
6. Serve with the marinara sauce

Nutrition per serving:

Calories – 456 | Fat - 11g | Carbs - 15g | Protein - 11g | Sugar – 2g | Fiber – 2g | Potassium - 240mg | Sodium – 410mg | Cholesterol – 45mg

4.5 Falafel Patties

Preparation Time: 5 mins |

Cooking Time: 8 mins | Serving: 2

Ingredients:
- Dressings:
- Salt and pepper – To taste
- Parsley – 1 tbsp (15 g)
- Oregano – 1 tbsp (15 g)
- Coriander – 1 tbsp (15 g)
- Garlic puree – 1 tbsp (15 ml)
- Soft cheese – 4 tbsp (60 g)
- Greek yogurt – 3 tbsp (45 g)
- Feta cheese – 1 oz (28 g)
- Cheese – 1 oz (28 g) (grated)
- Lemon - 1
- Onion - 1
- Oats – 5 oz (142 g)
- Chickpeas – 1 can

Method:
1. Blend the chickpeas, onion, lemon rind, garlic, and seasonings
2. Add the mixture to a bowl and add half the soft cheese, cheese, and the feta
3. Create patties with your hands and roll in the oats
4. Cook at 190°C (370°F) for 8 minutes
5. Combine the rest of the soft cheese, Greek yogurt, and lemon juice in a bowl for the serving sauce

Nutrition per serving:

Calories – 445 | Fat - 10g | Carbs - 19g | Protein - 12g | Sugar – 1g | Fiber – 5g | Potassium - 580mg | Sodium – 360mg | Cholesterol – 25mg

4.6 Mushroom Pasta

Preparation Time: 5 mins |

Cooking Time: 15 mins | Serving: 2

Ingredients:
- Mushrooms – 8 oz (228 g) (sliced)
- Pasta – 7 oz (198 g) (pasta)
- Onion – 1 (chopped)
- Garlic – 2 tsp (10 g) (minced)
- Salt – 1 tsp (5 g)
- Red pepper – ½ tsp (2.5 g) (flakes)
- Double cream – 2.6 oz (73 g) p
- Mascarpone cheese – 2.4 oz (68 g)
- Thyme – 1 tsp (5 g) (dried)
- Black pepper – 1 tsp (5 g) (ground)

Method:
1. Place all the ingredients in a bowl and mix well
2. Heat the air fryer to 160°C (320°F)
3. Grease a 7x3 inch pan and pour in the mixture
4. Place in the air fryer and cook for 15 minutes stirring halfway through
5. Pour over your cooked pasta

Nutrition per serving:

Calories – 450 | Fat - 19g | Carbs - 31g | Protein - 13g | Sugar – 3g | Fiber – 2.7g | Potassium - 280mg | Sodium – 340mg | Cholesterol – 52mg

4.7 Courgette Rolls

Preparation Time: 5 mins |

Cooking Time: 10 mins | Serving: 2

Ingredients:
- Oats – 14 oz (397 g)
- Feta – 1.4 oz (39 g) (crumbled)
- Egg – 1 (beaten)
- Courgetti – 5 oz (142 g) (grated)
- Lemon-1 tsp (5 g) (rind)
- Basil leaves - 6 (thinly sliced)
- Oregano – 1 tsp (5 g)
- Dill – 1 tsp (5 g)
- Salt and pepper – To taste

Method:
1. Place all ingredients in a bowl, except for the oats
2. Blend the oats until coarse
3. Add the oats and combine
4. Form into balls and place in the air fryer
5. Cook for 10 minutes at 200°C (390°F)

Nutrition per serving:

Calories – 400 | Fat - 19g | Carbs - 31g | Protein - 13g | Sugar – 2g | Fiber – 3.8g | Potassium - 230mg | Sodium – 410mg | Cholesterol – 98mg

4.8 Cheese & Pasta Quiche

Preparation Time: 5 mins |

Cooking Time: 20 mins | Serving: 2

Ingredients:
- Pastry – 1 packet (ready shortcrust)
- Pasta – 8 tbsp (120 g)
- Eggs - 2
- Cheese – 14 oz (396 g) (grated)
- Greek yogurt – 2 tbsp (30 g)
- Milk – 0.6 cups (141 ml)
- Garlic puree – 1 tsp (5 ml)
- Ramekin dishes – 4 (greased)

Method:
1. Line the ramekin dishes with the shortcrust pastry
2. Combine the yogurt, garlic, and macaroni
3. Spoon into the dishes until almost full
4. Mix the egg and milk together and pour over the pasta
5. Add the cheese and place in the air fryer
6. Cook at 190°C (370°F) for 20 minutes

Nutrition per serving:

Calories – 440 | Fat - 12g | Carbs - 30g | Protein - 4g | Sugar – 1g | Fiber – 1.5g | Potassium - 150mg | Sodium – 480mg | Cholesterol – 95mg

4.9 Lentil Balls

Preparation Time: 5 mins |

Cooking Time: 12 mins | Serving: 2

Ingredients:
- Lentils – 2 cans
- Rice – 7 oz (198 g)
- Water – 1.6 cups (378 ml)
- Walnut – 7 oz (198 g) (halves)
- Mushrooms – 3 tbsp (45 g) (dried)
- Parsley – 3 tbsp (45 g)
- Tomato – 1.5 tbsp (22.5 g) (paste)
- Breadcrumbs – 3.5 oz (99 g)
- Lemon – 2 tbsp (30 ml) (juice and zest)
- Salt and pepper – To taste

Method:
1. Blend the lentils, walnuts, mushrooms, parsley, tomato paste, salt, pepper in a food processor
2. Fold in the breadcrumbs
3. Create small balls and place in the air fryer at 200°C (390°F)
4. Cook for 10 minutes
5. Turn and cook for a further 5 minutes
6. Add the rice to a pan with water. Bring the mixture to the boil and turn down to a simmer for 20 minutes.
7. Add the lemon juice, lemon zest, and salt

Nutrition per serving:

Calories – 500 | Fat - 19g | Carbs - 18g | Protein - 13g | Sugar – 1g | Fiber – 7.8g | Potassium - 360mg | Sodium – 180mg | Cholesterol – 0mg

4.10 Air Fryer Vegetable Bake

Preparation Time: 5 mins |

Cooking Time: 10 mins | Serving: 2

Ingredients:
- Flour – 1 oz (28 g) (plain)
- Vegetable – 10 oz (284 g) packet (baked)

Method:
1. Preheat the air fryer to 200°C (390°F)
2. Mix the flour with the vegetable bake
3. Create ball shapes and arrange in the fryer
4. Cook for 10 minutes

Nutrition per serving:

Calories – 400 | Fat - 19g | Carbs - 31g | Protein - 13g | Sugar – 3g | Fiber – 5g | Potassium - 230mg | Sodium – 150mg | Cholesterol – 0mg

4.11 Mediterranean Gnocchi

Preparation Time: 5 mins |

Cooking Time: 10 mins | Serving: 2

Ingredients:
- Gnocchi – 1 packet (prepared)
- Olive oil – 2 tbsp (30 ml)
- Cherry tomatoes – 5 oz (142 g) (halves)
- Balsamic vinegar – 2 tbsp (30 ml)
- Garlic – 3 cloves (pressed)
- Basil – 7 oz (198 g) (chopped)
- Mozzarella balls – 7 oz (198 g) (mini)
- Salt and pepper – To taste

Method:
1. Combine the cherry tomatoes, gnocchi, oil, balsamic vinegar, garlic, and seasoning
2. Transfer to the air fryer basket and cook for 10 minutes at 200°C (390°F)
3. Once cooked, transfer everything to a large mixing bowl and add the mozzarella and basil

Nutrition per serving:
Calories – 590 | Fat - 21g | Carbs - 35g | Protein - 6g | Sugar – 2g | Fiber – 3g | Potassium - 180mg | Sodium – 270mg | Cholesterol – 25mg

4.12 Healthy Vegetarian Pizza

Preparation Time: 5 mins |

Cooking Time: 4 mins | Serving: 2

Ingredients:
- Wholewheat pitta breads - 2
- Marinara sauce – 3.5 oz (99 g)
- Baby spinach – 7 oz (198 g)
- Tomato – 1 (sliced)
- Clove garlic – 1 (sliced)
- Cheese – 14 oz (396 g) (grated)

Method:
1. Spread the marinara over each of the pittas
2. Sprinkle with cheese, top with spinach, plum tomato, and garlic
3. Place in the air fryer and cook for about 4 mins at 180°C (370°F)

Nutrition per serving:
Calories – 390 | Fat - 6g | Carbs - 10g | Protein - 6g | Sugar – 1g | Fiber – 4g | Potassium - 180mg | Sodium – 230mg | Cholesterol – 30mg

4.13 Air Fryer Tofu

Preparation Time: 5 mins |

Cooking Time: 8 mins | Serving: 2

Ingredients:
- Quinoa – 10 oz (284 g)
- Tofu – 1 block (cubed)
- Carrot – 1 (grated)
- Avocado – 1 (sliced)
- Onion – 1 (chopped)
- Soy sauce – 0.2 cups (47 ml)
- Sesame oil – 2 tbsp (30 ml)
- Garlic – 1tsp (5 g) (powder)
- Tahini – 2 tbsp (30 g) (dressing)
- Baby bok choy – 3 brunches (chopped)
- Cucumber – 1 (sliced)

Method:
1. Mix the soy sauce, 1 tbsp sesame oil, and garlic powder together
2. Add the tofu and place to one side for 10 minutes
3. Place in the air fryer and cook at 200°C (390°F) for 20 minutes - turning halfway
4. Heat the remaining sesame oil in a pan and cook the onions for about 4 minutes
5. Add the bok choy and cook for another 4 minutes
6. Divide the quinoa between your bowls and add bok choy, carrot, cucumber, and avocado.
7. Top with the tofu
8. Drizzle with Tahini

Nutrition per serving:

Calories – 200 | Fat - 3g | Carbs - 3g | Protein - 6g | Sugar – 1g | Fiber – 3g | Potassium - 120mg | Sodium – 360mg | Cholesterol – 0mg

4.14 Creamy Pasta Bake

Preparation Time: 5 mins |

Cooking Time: 20 mins | Serving: 2

Ingredients:
- Pasta – 5 oz (142 g) (any type)
- Cheese – 14 oz (400 g) (grated)
- Greek yogurt – 2 tbsp (30 g)
- Eggs - 2
- Milk – 0.6 cups (141 ml)
- Garlic – 1 tsp (5 g) (puree)
- Ramekin dishes – 4 greased

Method:
1. Rub the inside of 4 ramekins with flour
2. Mix the yogurt, garlic, and pasta together and place inside the ramekins
3. Mix the egg and milk together
4. Divide between the ramekins and top with cheese
5. Cook in the air fryer at 190°C (370°F) for 20 minutes

Nutrition per serving:

Calories – 450 | Fat - 18g | Carbs - 15g | Protein - 11g | Sugar – 1g | Fiber – 2g | Potassium - 210mg | Sodium – 280mg | Cholesterol – 90mg

4.15 Potato Gratin

Preparation Time: 5 mins |

Cooking Time: 20 mins | Serving: 2

Ingredients:
- Coconut cream – 0.5 cups (118 ml)
- Cheese – 1.7 oz (48 g) (grated)
- Potatoes – 2 (sliced thinly)
- Eggs – 2 (beaten)
- Flour – 1 tbsp (15 g)
- Ramekin dishes – 4 (greased)

Method:
1. Place the potatoes in the air fryer, and cook for 10 minutes at 360°F
2. Combine the eggs, coconut cream, and flour
3. Line four ramekins with the potato slices
4. Add the cream mixture
5. Sprinkle with cheese, and cook for 10 minutes at 200°C (390°F)

Nutrition per serving:

Calories – 400 | Fat - 19g | Carbs - 19g | Protein - 7g | Sugar – 1g | Fiber – 2g | Potassium - 190mg | Sodium – 250mg | Cholesterol – 90mg

5 VEGAN PLATE RECIPES

5.1 Artichoke & Pumpkin Seed Pasta

Preparation Time: 5 mins |

Cooking Time: 12 mins | Serving: 2

Ingredients:
- Pasta – 3.5 oz (99 g) (your choice)
- Artichoke hearts - 6
- Pumpkin seeds – 2 tbsp (30 g)
- Chickpeas – 1 can
- Basil leaves – 1.7 oz (48 g)
- Lemon juice – 2 tbsp (30 ml)
- Garlic – 1 clove
- Miso paste – 0.5 tsp (2.5 g)
- Olive oil – 1 tsp (5 ml)

Method:
1. Cook the chickpeas in the air fryer at 200°C (390°F) for 12 minutes
2. Meanwhile, cook your pasta on the stove to your liking and place in serving bowls
3. Add the remaining ingredients to a food processor and blend
4. Top the pasta with the pesto mix and roasted chickpeas

Nutrition per serving:

Calories – 400 | Fat - 5g | Carbs - 6g | Protein - 4g | Sugar – 1g | Fiber – 5g | Potassium - 700mg | Sodium – 150mg | Cholesterol – 0mg

5.2 Jackfruit Taquitos

Preparation Time: 5 mins |

Cooking Time: 25 mins | Serving: 2

Ingredients:
- Fresh or canned jackfruit - 1 cup (150 g)
- Wheat tortillas - 4
- Water – 1/4 cup (60 ml)
- Canned red beans – 8 oz (226 g), drained and rinsed
- Pico de Gallo sauce – 3.5 oz (99 g)
- Chili powder - 1 tsp (2.8 g)
- Cumin - 1/2 tsp (1.4 g)
- Garlic powder - 1/2 tsp (1.4 g)
- Salt - 1/4 tsp (0.6 g)
- Olive oil spray

Method:
1. If using fresh jackfruit, cook it in boiling water until tender, about 15-20 minutes. Drain and shred the jackfruit with a fork.
2. In a saucepan, combine the shredded jackfruit, red beans, water, Pico de Gallo sauce, chili powder, cumin, garlic powder, and salt. Bring to a boil, then reduce the heat and simmer for 10-15 minutes, stirring occasionally, until the mixture is thick, and the flavors have melded.
3. Preheat the air fryer to 180°C (350°F).
4. Mash the jackfruit mixture and add 1/4 cup of the mixture to each tortilla. Roll up tightly and place in the air fryer basket, seam-side down.
5. Spray the taquitos with olive oil spray.
6. Cook for 8-10 minutes, or until crispy and golden brown.
7. Serve hot with additional Pico de Gallo sauce, if desired.

Nutrition per serving:

Calories – 380 | Fat - 7g | Carbs - 4g | Protein - 7g | Sugar – 1g | Fiber – 6g | Potassium - 300mg | Sodium – 250mg | Cholesterol – 0mg

5.3 Air Fryer Pierogies

Preparation Time: 5 mins |

Cooking Time: 16 mins | Serving: 2

Ingredients:
- Olive oil – 1 tbsp (15 ml)
- Pierogies - 14
- Onion - 1 (sliced)
- Sugar – 1 tsp (5 g)

Method:
1. Bring a saucepan of water to the boil and cook the pierogis for 5 minutes
2. Drain and place to one side
3. Add a little oil to the basket and add the onion, cooking for 12 minutes at 200°C (390°F)
4. After 5 minutes have passed, add the sugar
5. Remove the onions and place to one side
6. Add the dumplings to the air fryer and cook for 4 minutes
7. Mix the dumplings with the onions before serving

Nutrition per serving:

Calories – 690 | Fat - 19g | Carbs - 31g | Protein - 13g | Sugar – 3g | Fiber – 4g | Potassium - 180mg | Sodium – 600mg | Cholesterol – 25mg

5.4 Radish Browns

Preparation Time: 5 mins |

Cooking Time: 13 mins | Serving: 2

Ingredients:
- Salt and pepper – To taste
- Paprika – ½ tsp (2.5 g)
- Onion powder – ½ tsp (2.5 g)
- Onion – 1 (chopped)
- Coconut oil – 1 tsp (5 g)
- Radish – 10 oz (284 g) (trimmed and chopped)

Method:
1. Place the onions and radish in a bowl with the coconut oil and combine
2. Place in the air fryer and cook at 180°C (370°F) for 8 minutes, shaking halfway through
3. Add seasoning and cook for another 5 minutes

Nutrition per serving:

Calories – 360 | Fat - 11g | Carbs - 15g | Protein - 10g | Sugar – 1g | Fiber – 3g | Potassium - 230mg | Sodium – 400mg | Cholesterol – 0mg

5.5 Lentil & Cabbage Patties

Preparation Time: 5 mins |

Cooking Time: 35 mins | Serving: 2

Ingredients:
- Black lentils – 3.5 oz (99 g)
- White cabbage – 3.5 oz (99 g)
- Carrot – 1 (grated)
- Onion – 1 (diced and blended)
- Oats – 10.5 oz (284 g)
- Garlic puree – 1 tbsp (15 ml)
- Cumin – 1 tsp (5 g)
- Salt and pepper – To taste

Method:
1. Cook the lentils in a pan with water for 45 minutes
2. Combine all ingredients in a bowl and use your hands to create burgers
3. Place in the air fryer and cook at 180°C (370°F) for 30 minutes

Nutrition per serving:

Calories – 400 | Fat - 3g | Carbs - 15g | Protein - 9g | Sugar – 1g | Fiber – 8g | Potassium - 170mg | Sodium – 420mg | Cholesterol – 0mg

5.6 Courgette & Coriander Burgers

Preparation Time: 5 mins |

Cooking Time: 12 mins | Serving: 2

Ingredients:
- Dressings:
- Salt and pepper – To taste
- Chili powder – 1 tsp (5 g)
- Mixed spice – 1tsp (5 g)
- Coriander – 3 tbsp (45 g)
- Cumin – 1 tsp (5 g)
- Courgette – 1 (grated)
- Spring onions – 3 (sliced)
- Chickpeas – 1 can (drained)

Method:
1. Take a large bowl and combine the grated courgette, drained chickpeas, and the sliced spring onions
2. Season to your liking and use your hands to create burgers
3. Cook in the air fryer for 12 minutes at 200°C (390°F)

Nutrition per serving:

Calories – 440 | Fat - 5g | Carbs - 18g | Protein - 8g | Sugar – 1g | Fiber – 6g | Potassium - 270mg | Sodium – 410mg | Cholesterol – 0mg

5.7 Vegan Cheese with Bread Sticks

Preparation Time: 5 mins |

Cooking Time: 12 mins | Serving: 2

Ingredients:
- Bread – 2 slices
- Vegan cheese – 1 piece
- Mustard – 1 tbsp (15 g)

Method:
1. Cook the cheese in the air fryer for 15 minutes at 190°C (370°F)
2. Meanwhile, toast your bread and cut into stripes
3. Place the cheese on top of the bread and serve with the mustard

Nutrition per serving:

Calories – 490 | Fat - 15g | Carbs - 19g | Protein - 11g | Sugar – 2g | Fiber – 2g | Potassium - 190mg | Sodium – 370mg | Cholesterol – 0mg

5.8 Canarian Potatoes

Preparation Time: 5 mins |

Cooking Time: 23 mins | Serving: 2

Ingredients:
- Olive oil – 1 tsp (5 g)
- Potatoes – 4 (wedges)
- Taco – 1 tsp (5 g) (seasoning)
- Paprika – 2 tsp (10 g)
- Dried garlic – 2 tsp (10 g)
- Salt and pepper – To taste

Method:
1. Place the potatoes and olive oil in a bowl with the seasoning and combine
2. Add to the air fryer and cook at 370°F for 20 minutes
3. Shake and turn the air fryer up to 200°C (390°F). Cook for another 3 minutes

Nutrition per serving:

Calories – 390 | Fat - 14g | Carbs - 20g | Protein - 7g | Sugar – 2g | Fiber – 3g | Potassium - 390mg | Sodium – 420mg | Cholesterol – 0mg

5.9 Cheesy Bagel Pizza

Preparation Time: 5 mins |

Cooking Time: 7 mins | Serving: 2

Ingredients:
- Uncooked bagel - 1 (cut in half)
- Vegan pepperoni – 6 slices
- Vegan cheese – 2 slices
- Marinara sauce – 2 tbsp (30 g)
- Basil – 1 pinch

Method:
1. Toast the bagel at 190°C (370°F) for 2 minutes in the air fryer
2. Add the marinara sauce, pepperoni, and cheese
3. Return to the air fryer and cook for 5 minutes
4. Sprinkle with basil

Nutrition per serving:

Calories – 690 | Fat - 19g | Carbs - 31g | Protein - 13g | Sugar – 3g | Fiber – 4g | Potassium - 190mg | Sodium – 710mg | Cholesterol – 0mg

5.10 Pumpkin & Lemon Pasta

Preparation Time: 5 mins |

Cooking Time: 5 mins | Serving: 2

Ingredients:
- Pasta – 3.5 oz (99 g)
- Basil leaves – 1.7 oz (48 g)
- Pumpkin seeds – 2 tbsp (30 g)
- Lemon juice – 2 tbsp (30 ml)
- Garlic – 1 clove

Method:
1. Cook the pasta according to packet instructions
2. Add the remaining ingredients to a food processor and blend
3. Add the pasta the mixture and place in the air fryer for 5 minutes at 190°C (370°F)

Nutrition per serving:

Calories – 500 | Fat - 15g | Carbs - 14g | Protein - 6g | Sugar – 1g | Fiber – 3.5g | Potassium - 680mg | Sodium – 15mg | Cholesterol – 0mg

5.11 Crostini with Artichoke

Preparation Time: 5 mins |

Cooking Time: 4 mins | Serving: 2

Ingredients:
- Olive oil – 1 tbsp (1 ml)
- Baguette – 1 (slices)
- Artichoke hearts – 7 oz (198 g) (grilled)
- Cashews – 3.5 oz (99 g)
- Lemon juice – 1 tbsp (15 ml)
- Balsamic vinegar – 1 tsp (5 ml)
- Basil – 0.5 tsp (2.5 g)
- Garlic – 1 clove (minced)
- Salt and pepper – To taste

Method:
1. Combine cashews, olive oil, lemon juice, balsamic vinegar, basil oregano, onion powder, garlic, and salt in a bowl. Set aside
2. Place the baguette slices in the air fryer and cook at 190°C (370°F) for 3-4 minutes
3. Sprinkle the baguette slices with cashew mix then add the artichoke hearts

Nutrition per serving:
Calories – 440 | Fat - 10g | Carbs - 3g | Protein - 9g | Sugar – 2g | Fiber – 4g | Potassium - 190mg | Sodium – 320mg | Cholesterol – 0mg

5.12 Cheesy Baked Potato

Preparation Time: 5 mins |

Cooking Time: 40 mins | Serving: 2

Ingredients:
- Potato – 1 (baking)
- Oil – 1 tsp (5 ml)
- Onion powder – 0.25 tsp (1.25 ml)
- Vegan butter – 1 tbsp (15 g)
- Vegan cream cheese – 1 tbsp (15 g)
- Olives – 1 tbsp (15 g)
- Chives – 1 tsp (5 g)
- Salt and pepper – To taste

Method:
1. Prick the potato with a fork and lightly coat the surface with oil. Season with salt and onion powder.
2. Place the potato in the air fryer and cook at 200°C (390°F) for 40 minutes.
3. In a bowl, mix the vegan butter, vegan cream cheese, olives, and chives. Serve this mixture on top of the baked potato once it is cooked.

Nutrition per serving:
Calories – 330 | Fat - 20g | Carbs - 32g | Protein - 5g | Sugar – 2g | Fiber – 4g | Potassium - 800mg | Sodium – 250mg | Cholesterol – 0mg

5.13 BBQ Soy Curls

Preparation Time: 5 mins |

Cooking Time: 5 mins | Serving: 2

Ingredients:
- Water – 1 cup (235 ml)
- Soy curls – 7 oz (198 g)
- BBQ sauce – 1.4 oz (39 g)
- Vegetable bouillon – 1 tsp (5 ml)

Method:
1. Soak the soy curls in water and bouillon for 10 minutes before shredding
2. Cook in the air fryer for 3 minutes at 200°C (390°F)
3. Remove from the air fryer and coat in bbq sauce
4. Return to the air fryer and cook for 5 minutes

Nutrition per serving:

Calories – 190 | Fat - 5g | Carbs - 9g | Protein - 6g | Sugar – 2g | Fiber – 3g | Potassium - 450mg | Sodium – 450mg | Cholesterol – 0mg

5.14 Onion Arancini

Preparation Time: 5 mins |

Cooking Time: 12 mins | Serving: 2

Ingredients:
- Risotto – ½ packet
- Breadcrumbs – 3.5 oz (99 g)
- Onion powder – 1 tsp (5 g)
- Marinara sauce – 1.2 cups (283 g) (pre-warmed)
- Salt and pepper – To taste

Method:
1. Form a rice ball with the risotto
2. Mix the breadcrumbs, onion powder, salt, and pepper
3. Coat the risotto ball in the crumb mix
4. Place in the air fryer, spray with oil, and cook at 200°C (390°F) for 10 minutes
5. Serve with warm marinara sauce

Nutrition per serving:

Calories – 690 | Fat - 19g | Carbs - 31g | Protein - 13g | Sugar – 3g | Fiber – 2g | Potassium - 430mg | Sodium – 550mg | Cholesterol – 5mg

5.15 Sweet Potato Wraps

Preparation Time: 5 mins |

Cooking Time: 24 mins | Serving: 2

Ingredients:
- Sweet potato – 1 (cubed)
- Water – 3 tbsp (45 ml)
- Corn tortillas - 3
- Black beans – 14 oz (396 g)
- Olive oil – 1 tsp (5 ml)
- Onion – 1 (chopped)
- Garlic – 1 tsp (5 g) (minced)
- Chipotle pepper - 1 (chopped)
- Cumin – 0.5 tsp (2.5 g)
- Paprika – 0.5 tsp (2.5 g)
- Chili powder – 0.5 tsp (1.25 g)
- Salt and pepper – To taste

Method:
1. Place the sweet potato in the air fryer spray and cook for 12 minutes at 200°C (390°F)
2. Heat oil in a pan, add the onion and garlic, and cook for a few minutes until soft
3. Add remaining ingredients to the pan, add 2 tbsp of water and combine
4. Add the sweet potato and 1 tbsp of water and mix
5. Warm the tortilla in the microwave for about 1 minute
6. Place a row of filling across the center of each tortilla. Fold up the tortilla
7. Place in the air fryer and cook for about 12 minutes

Nutrition per serving:

Calories – 400 | Fat - 9g | Carbs - 10g | Protein - 7g | Sugar – 2g | Fiber – 6g | Potassium - 210mg | Sodium – 290mg | Cholesterol – 0mg

6 SIDE DISH RECIPES

6.1 Crunchy Ranch Potatoes

Preparation Time: 5 mins |

Cooking Time: 15 mins | Serving: 2

Ingredients:
- Olive oil – 1 tbsp (15 ml)
- Baby potatoes – 10 oz (284 g)
- Dry ranch – 3 tbsp (45 g) (seasoning)

Method:
1. Take a mixing bowl and combine the olive oil with the ranch seasoning
2. Add the potatoes to the bowl and toss to coat
3. Cook for 15 minutes at 200°C (390°F), shaking halfway through

Nutrition per serving:

Calories – 390 | Fat - 4g | Carbs - 8g | Protein - 4g | Sugar – 1g | Fiber – 1.5g | Potassium - 300mg | Sodium – 400mg | Cholesterol – 0mg

6.2 Cheesy Carrot Chips

Preparation Time: 5 mins |

Cooking Time: 20 mins | Serving: 2

Ingredients:
- Olive oil – 1 tbsp (15 ml)
- Carrots – 6 oz (170 g) (halved)
- Garlic clove – 1 (crushed)
- Parmesan – 2 tbsp (30 g) (grated)
- Salt and pepper – To taste

Method:
1. Combine the olive oil and garlic
2. Add the carrots to the bowl and toss well
3. Add the parmesan and coat the carrots well
4. Add to the air fryer and cook for 20 minutes at 200°C (390°F), shaking at the halfway point

Nutrition per serving:

Calories – 300 | Fat - 9g | Carbs - 10g | Protein - 7g | Sugar – 1g | Fiber – 2.5g | Potassium - 320mg | Sodium – 250mg | Cholesterol – 10mg

6.3 Spicy Rice

Preparation Time: 5 mins |

Cooking Time: 50 mins | Serving: 2

Ingredients:
- Olive oil – 3 tbsp (45 ml)
- Long grain rice – 17 oz (481 g) (washed)
- Onion – 1 (chopped)
- Chicken stock – 2 cups (475 ml)
- Water – 0.25 cups (118 ml)
- Chili powder – 1 tsp (5 g)
- Cumin – 0.25 tsp (1 g)
- Tomato paste – 2 tbsp (30 g)
- Garlic powder – 0.5 tsp (2.5 g)
- Red pepper flakes – 1 tsp (5 g)
- Jalapeño pepper – ½ small (chopped)
- Salt and pepper – to taste

Method:
1. Add the water and tomato paste and combine, placing to one side
2. Take a baking pan and add a little oil
3. Place the rice on the baking pan
4. Add the chicken stock, tomato paste, jalapeños, onions, and the rest of the olive oil, and combine
5. Place tin foil over the top and place it in your air fryer
6. Cook at 200°C (390°F) for 50 minutes

Nutrition per serving:

Calories – 400 | Fat - 3g | Carbs – 9g | Protein - 6g | Sugar – 1g | Fiber – 1.8g | Potassium - 50mg | Sodium – 410mg | Cholesterol – 0mg

6.4 Garlic Asparagus

Preparation Time: 5 mins |

Cooking Time: 10 mins | Serving: 2

Ingredients:
- Olive oil – 1 tsp (5 ml)
- Asparagus – 17 oz (481 g)
- Garlic salt – 1 tsp (5 g)
- Parmesan cheese – 1 tbsp (15 g) (grated)
- Salt and pepper – to taste

Method:
1. Place the asparagus in the air fryer with the oil
2. Sprinkle the parmesan and garlic salt on top, and season
3. Cook for between 7 and 10 minutes at 180°C (370°F)

Nutrition per serving:

Calories – 200 | Fat - 9g | Carbs - 10g | Protein - 7g | Sugar – 1g | Fiber – 3.5g | Potassium - 210mg | Sodium – 520mg | Cholesterol – 4mg

6.5 Tasty Potato Wedges

Preparation Time: 5 mins |

Cooking Time: 18 mins | Serving: 2

Ingredients:
- Potatoes – 2 (wedges)
- Olive oil – 1.5 tbsp (22.5 ml)
- Chili powder – 0.5 tsp (2.5 g)
- Paprika – 0.5 tsp (2.5 g)
- Salt and pepper – To taste

Method:
1. Add all ingredients to a bowl and combine well
2. Place the wedges into the air fryer and cook for 10 minutes at 200°C (390°F)
3. Turn and cook for a further 8 minutes

Nutrition per serving:
Calories – 210 | Fat - 9g | Carbs - 15g | Protein - 4g | Sugar – 1g | Fiber – 2.2g | Potassium - 220mg | Sodium – 150mg | Cholesterol – 0mg

6.6 Avocado Chips

Preparation Time: 5 mins |

Cooking Time: 7 mins | Serving: 2

Ingredients:
- Egg - 1
- Avocado – 1 (sliced)
- Breadcrumbs – 3.5 oz (99 g)
- Flour – 5 oz (142 g)
- Water – 1 tsp (5 ml)
- Salt and pepper – To taste

Method:
1. Mix flour salt and pepper together in a bowl
2. Beat egg and water together in another bowl and add breadcrumbs to a third
3. Dip the avocado into the flour, then the egg then into the breadcrumbs
4. Spray with cooking oil and place in the air fryer
5. Cook for 4 minutes at 200°C (390°F), turn then cook for a further 3 minutes

Nutrition per serving:
Calories – 380 | Fat - 5g | Carbs - 4g | Protein - 7g | Sugar – 1g | Fiber – 5.5g | Potassium - 390mg | Sodium – 80mg | Cholesterol – 94mg

6.7 Fruity Tofu

Preparation Time: 5 mins |

Cooking Time: 10 mins | Serving: 2

Ingredients:
- Tofu – 14 oz (396 g) (drained and cubes)
- Maple syrup – 1 Tbsp (15 ml)
- Orange juice – 0.3 cups (80 ml)
- Cornstarch – 2 tsp (10 g)
- Tamari – 1 tbsp (15 ml)
- Cornstarch – 1 tbsp (10 g)
- Pepper flakes – 1/4 tsp (0.5 g)
- Orange juice – 0.3 cups (70 ml)
- Orange zest – 1 tsp (5 g)
- Ginger – 1 tsp (5 g) (minced)
- Garlic – 1 tsp (5 g)
- Water – 1/3 cups (80 ml)

Method:
1. Place the tofu in a bowl add the tamari, combine
2. Mix in 1 tbsp starch and allow to sit for 30 minutes
3. Place the remaining ingredients into another bowl and mix well
4. Place the tofu in the air fryer and cook at 180°C (370°F) for about 10 minutes
5. Add tofu to a pan with the sauce mixture and cook until the sauce thickens

Nutrition per serving:

Calories – 190 | Fat - 2g | Carbs - 7g | Protein - 3g | Sugar – 1g | Fiber – 0.5g | Potassium - 400mg | Sodium – 380mg | Cholesterol – 0mg

6.8 Parsley Courgette

Preparation Time: 5 mins |

Cooking Time: 15 mins | Serving: 2

Ingredients:
- Courgettes – 2
- Vegetable oil – 1 tbsp (15 ml)
- Parsley – 1 tbsp (15 g) (chopped)
- Breadcrumbs – 2 tbsp (30 g)
- Grated parmesan – 4 tbsp (60 g)
- Salt and pepper – To taste

Method:
1. Preheat the air fryer to 180°C (350°F).
2. Combine all ingredients except for the courgette in a bowl.
3. Place the courgette in the air fryer and evenly sprinkle the breadcrumb mixture on top.
4. Cook for approximately 15 minutes at 180°C (350°F).

Nutrition per serving:

Calories – 290 | Fat - 9g | Carbs - 4g | Protein - 3g | Sugar – 1g | Fiber – 1.2g | Potassium - 250mg | Sodium – 180mg | Cholesterol – 7mg

6.9 Stuffed Pumpkin

Preparation Time: 5 mins |

Cooking Time: 30 mins | Serving: 2

Ingredients:
- Pumpkin – ½ (seeds removed)
- 1 egg - 1
- Sweet potato – 1 (chopped)
- Parsnip – 1 (chopped)
- 1 Onion – 1 (chopped)
- carrot – 1 (chopped)
- Dried mixed herbs – 2 tsp (10 g)
- Peas – 1 oz (28 g)
- Garlic cloves – 2 (minced)

Method:
1. Combine all ingredients in a bowl, except for the pumpkin
2. Stuff the pumpkin with the mixture
3. Place the pumpkin in the air fryer and cook for about 30 minutes at 180°C (370°F)

Nutrition per serving:

Calories – 180 | Fat - 7g | Carbs - 9g | Protein - 6g | Sugar – 1g | Fiber – 4.5g | Potassium - 800mg | Sodium – 120mg | Cholesterol – 95mg

6.10 Marinated Cauliflower

Preparation Time: 5 mins |

Cooking Time: 24 mins | Serving: 2

Ingredients:
- Water – 0.4 cups (94 ml)
- Cauliflower – 1 small (florets)
- Onion – 1 (sliced)
- Cornstarch – 1 oz (28 g)
- Flour – 1.7 oz (48 g)
- Tomato ketchup – 2 tbsp (30 g)
- Brown sugar – 2 tbsp (30 g)
- Salt and pepper – To taste

Method:
1. Mix together flour, cornstarch, water, salt, and pepper until smooth
2. Coat the cauliflower and chill for 30 minutes
3. Place in the air fryer and cook for 22 minutes at 180°C (370°F)
4. Meanwhile combine remaining ingredients in a saucepan, gently simmer until thickened.
5. Serve the cauliflower with the sauce on top.

Nutrition per serving:

Calories – 190 | Fat - 4g | Carbs - 9g | Protein - 5g | Sugar – 2g | Fiber – 3.2g | Potassium - 300mg | Sodium – 220mg | Cholesterol – 0mg

7 POULTRY RECIPES

7.1 Turkey in Mushroom Sauce

Preparation Time: 5 mins |

Cooking Time: 21 mins | Serving: 2

Ingredients:
- Mushroom soup – 1 can
- Milk – 0.6 cups (141 ml)
- Turkey – 2 cutlets
- Butter – 1 tbsp (15 g)
- Salt and pepper – To taste

Method:
1. Brush the turkey cutlets with the butter and seasoning
2. Place in the air fryer and cook for 11 minutes at 200°C (390°F)
3. Add the mushroom soup and milk to a pan and cook over the stove for around 10 minutes, stirring every so often
4. Pour the sauce over the cutlets

Nutrition per serving:

Calories – 426 | Fat - 21g | Carbs - 18g | Protein - 5g | Sugar – 1g | Fiber – 0.8g | Potassium - 260mg | Sodium – 420mg | Cholesterol – 58mg

7.2 Zingy Lemon Chicken Wings

Preparation Time: 5 mins |

Cooking Time: 26 mins | Serving: 2

Ingredients:
- Chicken wings – 2.2 lb (997 g)
- Cayenne pepper – ¼ tbsp
- Lemon pepper – 2 tsp (10 g) (seasoning) and 1 tsp (5 g) (sauce)
- Butter – 3 tbsp (45 g)
- Honey – 1 tsp (5 g)

Method:
1. Preheat the air fryer to 180°C (350°F)
2. In a bowl, mix together the lemon pepper seasoning and cayenne pepper.
3. Coat the chicken wings evenly with the seasoning mixture.
4. Place the chicken wings in the air fryer and cook for 20 minutes, turning them over halfway through the cooking time.
5. Increase the temperature to 200°C (390°F) and cook for another 6 minutes.
6. While the wings are cooking, melt the butter and combine it with the honey and the remaining lemon pepper seasoning.
7. Remove the wings from the air fryer and drizzle the sauce over the top.

Nutrition per serving:

Calories – 356 | Fat - 6g | Carbs - 31g | Protein - 7g | Sugar – 3g | Fiber – 1.2g | Potassium - 120mg | Sodium – 330mg | Cholesterol – 85mg

7.3 Air Fryer Potatoes with Chicken

Preparation Time: 5 mins |

Cooking Time: 20 mins | Serving: 2

Ingredients:
- Olive oil – 2 tbsp (30 ml)
- Potatoes - 2
- Chicken breast – 2 (chunks)
- Garlic cloves – 4 (crushed)
- Smoked paprika – 2 tsp (10 g)
- Thyme – 1 tsp (5 g)
- Red chili flakes – 0.5 tsp (2.5 g)
- Salt and pepper – To taste

Method:
1. Combine the potatoes with half of the garlic, half the paprika, half the chili flakes, salt, pepper, and half the oil
2. Place into the air fryer and cook for 5 minutes at 180°C (370°F), before turning over and cooking for another 5 minutes
3. Take a bowl and add the chicken with the rest of the seasonings and oil, until totally coated
4. Add the chicken to the potato's mixture, moving the potatoes to the side
5. Cook for 10 minutes, turning the chicken halfway through

Nutrition per serving:

Calories – 390 | Fat - 16g | Carbs - 21g | Protein - 7g | Sugar – 1g | Fiber – 2.6g | Potassium - 350mg | Sodium – 340mg | Cholesterol – 60mg

7.4 Spicy Tandoori Chicken

Preparation Time: 5 mins |

Cooking Time: 15 mins | Serving: 2

Ingredients:
- Chicken tenders – 17 oz (481 g) (halves)
- Minced ginger – 1 tbsp (15 g)
- Minced garlic - 1 tbsp (15 g)
- Cayenne pepper – 1 tsp (5 g)
- Turmeric – 1 tsp (5 g)
- Garam masala – 1 tsp (5 g)
- Yogurt – 0.3 cups (70 ml)
- Coriander leaves – 0.8 oz (22 g)
- Salt and pepper – to taste

Method:
1. Combine all the ingredients, except the chicken
2. Once combined, add the chicken to the bowl and make sure it is fully coated
3. Preheat the air fryer to 180°C (370°F) and cook the chicken for 10 minutes
4. Turnover and cook for another 5 minutes

Nutrition per serving:

Calories – 500 | Fat - 4g | Carbs - 19g | Protein - 8g | Sugar – 2g | Fiber – 2.1g | Potassium - 210mg | Sodium – 250mg | Cholesterol – 80mg

7.5 Turkey and Mushroom Burgers

Preparation Time: 5 mins |

Cooking Time: 10 mins | Serving: 2

Ingredients:
- Mushrooms – 6 oz (170 g)
- Minced turkey - 17 oz (481 g)
- Chicken seasoning – 1 tbsp (15 g)
- Onion powder - 1 tsp (5 g)
- Garlic powder - 1 tsp (5 g)
- Salt and pepper – to taste

Method:
1. Puree the mushrooms in a food processor
2. Add all the seasonings and mix well
3. Transfer the mixture to a mixing bowl
4. Add the minced turkey and combine again
5. Shape the mix into 5 patties
6. Spray with cooking spray and place in the air fryer
7. Cook at 180°C (370°F) for 10 minutes, until cooked

Nutrition per serving:

Calories – 360 | Fat - 10g | Carbs - 19g | Protein - 5g | Sugar – 2g | Fiber – 1.4g | Potassium - 290mg | Sodium – 280mg | Cholesterol – 85mg

7.6 Smoked Chicken

Preparation Time: 5 mins |

Cooking Time: 20 mins | Serving: 2

Ingredients:
- Chicken breasts – 2 (halved)
- Olive oil – 2 tsp (10 ml)
- Ground thyme – 1 tsp (5 g)
- Paprika – 2 tsp (10 g)
- Cumin – 1 tsp (5 g)
- Cayenne pepper 0.5 tsp (2.5 g)
- Onion powder 0.5 tsp (2.5 g)
- Salt and pepper – to taste

Method:
1. Combine the spices together
2. Pour the spice mixture onto a plate
3. Take each chicken breast and coat in the spices, pressing down to ensure an even distribution
4. Place the chicken to one side for 5 minutes
5. Preheat your air fryer to 180°C (370°F)
6. Arrange the chicken inside the fryer and cook for 10 minutes
7. Turn the chicken over and cook for another 10 minutes
8. Remove from the fryer and allow to sit for 5 minutes before serving

Nutrition per serving:

Calories – 432 | Fat - 4g | Carbs - 9g | Protein - 5g | Sugar – 2g | Fiber – 0.8g | Potassium - 210mg | Sodium – 220mg | Cholesterol – 80mg

7.7 Chicken Thighs in Bacon

Preparation Time: 1 hour |

Cooking Time: 20 mins | Serving: 2

Ingredients:
- Butter – 2.6 oz (73 g) (softened)
- Bacon – 3.5 oz (99 g)
- Boneless chicken thighs – 12 oz (340 g)
- Clove garlic – 0.5 (minced)
- Thyme – 0.25 tsp (1.25 g) (dried)
- Basil – 0.25 tsp (1.25 g) (dried)
- Salt and pepper – to taste

Method:
1. Mix the softened butter, garlic, thyme, basil, salt, and pepper.
2. Spread the butter mixture onto a sheet of plastic wrap and roll it up to form a log shape.
3. Refrigerate the butter log for at least 1 hour, then remove the plastic wrap.
4. Lay one bacon strip on a flat surface and place the chicken thigh on top of the bacon.
5. Add a slice of the cold butter log in the center of the chicken thigh and fold one end of the bacon over the chicken.
6. Fold the chicken thigh over, wrapping the bacon around it completely.
7. Cook the bacon-wrapped chicken thighs in the air fryer at 180°C (350°F) until the chicken is cooked through and the juices run clear.

Nutrition per serving:

Calories – 390 | Fat - 12g | Carbs - 18g | Protein - 9g | Sugar – 1g | Fiber – 0.6g | Potassium - 300mg | Sodium – 510mg | Cholesterol – 85mg

7.8 Chicken with a Bang!

Preparation Time: 5 mins |

Cooking Time: 15 mins | Serving: 2

Ingredients:
- Chicken breast - 17 oz (481 g)
- Egg - 1 (beaten)
- Milk - 0.2 cups (47 ml)
- Hot pepper sauce - 1 tbsp (15 ml)
- Flour - 2 oz (56 g)
- Tapioca starch – 2.4 oz (68 g)
- Seasoned salt – 1.5 tsp (7.5 g)
- Garlic granules - 1 tsp (5 g)
- Cumin – 0.5 tsp (2.5 g)
- Greek yogurt – 6 tbsp (90 g)
- Sweet chili sauce – 3 tbsp (45 ml)
- Hot sauce – 1 tsp (5 ml)

Method:
1. Take a mixing bowl and combine the egg, milk, and hot pepper sauce.
2. In another bowl, combine the flour, tapioca starch, seasoned salt, garlic granules, and cumin.
3. Dip the chicken pieces into the egg mixture and then into the flour mixture.
4. Place the chicken into the air fryer at 180°C (350°F) and cook for 15 minutes.
5. While cooking, mix together the Greek yogurt, sweet chili sauce, and hot sauce and serve with the chicken.

Nutrition per serving:

Calories – 450 | Fat - 17g | Carbs - 22g | Protein - 9g | Sugar – 2g | Fiber – 1.1g | Potassium - 290mg | Sodium – 470mg | Cholesterol – 90mg

7.9 Chicken Fried Rice

Preparation Time: 5 mins |

Cooking Time: 20 mins | Serving: 2

Nutrition per serving: calories - 390, fat 7g, carbs 13g, protein 10g, sugar 1g, potassium 260mg

Ingredients:

- White rice – 14 oz (396 g) (cooked)
- Cooked chicken – 14 oz (396 g) (pieces)
- Peas and carrots mix – 7 oz (198 g)
- Onion – 1 (diced)
- Soy sauce – 6 tbsp (90 ml)
- Vegetable oil – 1 tbsp (15 ml)

Method:

1. Combine the rice, vegetable oil, and soy sauce
2. Add the peas, carrots, diced onion, and the chicken and mix together well
3. Pour the mixture into a nonstick pan and place in the air fryer
4. Cook at 190°C (370°F) for 20 minutes

Nutrition per serving:

Calories – 390 | Fat - 7g | Carbs - 63g | Protein - 10g | Sugar – 1g | Fiber – 2.5g | Potassium - 260mg | Sodium – 570mg | Cholesterol – 40mg

7.10 Sticky Chicken Thighs

Preparation Time: 1 hour |

Cooking Time: 12 mins | Serving: 2

Ingredients:

- Chicken thighs - 7
- Buttermilk – 0.8 cups (189 ml)
- Maple syrup - ½ tbsp (7.5 ml)
- Egg - 1
- Garlic salt – 1 tsp (5 g)
- All-purpose flour – 4.9 oz (138 g)
- Tapioca flour – 2.2 oz (62 g)
- Sweet paprika – 1 tsp (5 g)
- Onion powder – 1 tsp (5 g)
- Black pepper – 0.25 tsp (1 g)
- Cayenne pepper – 0.25 tsp (1 g)
- Granulated garlic – 0.5 tsp (2.5 g)
- Honey powder – 0.5 tsp (2.5 g)

Method:

1. Combine the buttermilk, maple syrup, egg, and garlic powder
2. Transfer to a bag and add chicken thighs, shaking to combine well
3. Set aside for 1 hour
4. Take a shallow bowl and add the flour, tapioca flour, salt, sweet paprika, smoked paprika, pepper, cayenne pepper, and honey powder, combining well
5. Preheat the air fryer to 160°C (320°F)
6. Drag the chicken through the flour mixture and place the chicken skin side down in the air fryer
7. Cook for 12 minutes, until white in the middle

Nutrition per serving:

Calories – 550 | Fat - 13g | Carbs - 19g | Protein - 8g | Sugar – 2g | Fiber – 1.3g | Potassium - 210mg | Sodium – 450mg | Cholesterol – 120mg

7.11 Cayenne Wings

Preparation Time: 10 mins |

Cooking Time: 26 mins | Serving: 2

Ingredients:
- Chicken wings – 2 lb (910 g)
- Honey – 1 tsp (5 g)
- Cayenne pepper – 0.25 tsp (1 g)
- Lemon pepper – 2 tsp (10 g) (seasoning)
- Melted butter – 3 tbsp (45 g)

Method:
1. Preheat your air fryer to 160°C (320°F)
2. Take a bowl and mix together the cayenne and lemon pepper
3. Add the chicken and coat everything well
4. Place inside the air fryer and cook for 10 minutes on each side
5. Increase the temperature to 200°C (390°F) and cook for another 6 minutes
6. Mix the honey and melted butter together and pour over the chicken once cooked.

Nutrition per serving:

Calories – 730 | Fat - 53g | Carbs - 7g | Protein - 49g | Sugar – 6g | Fiber – 0.5g | Potassium - 440mg | Sodium – 850mg | Cholesterol – 220mg

7.12 Easy Chicken Nuggets

Preparation Time: 5 mins |

Cooking Time: 12 mins | Serving: 4

Ingredients:
- 8 Chicken tenders - 12 ounces (8 tenders x 1.5 ounces per tender) or 340 grams (8 tenders x 42.5 grams per tender)
- Breadcrumbs – 8 oz (226 g)
- Egg – 1 (beaten)
- Olive oil – 2 tbsp (30 ml)

Method:
1. Mix together the oil and breadcrumbs in a large bowl
2. Dip each tender in the egg, and then the breadcrumbs, coating evenly
3. Place inside the air fryer
4. Repeat with all tenders
5. Cook for 12 minutes at 180°C (360°F)

Nutrition per serving:

Calories – 213 | Fat - 26g | Carbs - 9g | Protein - 26g | Sugar – 3g | Fiber – 0.8g | Potassium - 50mg | Sodium – 250mg | Cholesterol – 60mg

7.13 Chicken & Jalapeño Chimichangas

Preparation Time: 5 mins |

Cooking Time: 12 mins | Serving: 6

Ingredients:
- Tortillas – 6 (flour)
- Cooked chicken – 3.5 oz (99 g) (shredded)
- Jalapeño pepper – 0.2 oz (5.6 g)
- Refried beans – 0.2 oz (5.6 g)
- Nacho cheese 0.5 oz (14 g)
- Cumin – 1 tsp (5 g)
- Chili powder – 0.5 tsp (2.5 g)
- Salsa – 5 tbsp (75 g)
- Salt and pepper – to taste

Method:
1. Take a large bowl and combine all ingredients, except the tortillas
2. Place a little of the filling into each tortilla and roll up, sealing the edges
3. Place inside the air fryer
4. Cook at 200°C (390°F) for 7 minutes

Nutrition per serving:

Calories – 406 | Fat - 21g | Carbs - 26g | Protein - 26g | Sugar – 4g | Fiber – 3g | Potassium - 55mg | Sodium – 450mg | Cholesterol – 60mg

7.14 Paprika & Garlic Chicken

Preparation Time: 10 mins |

Cooking Time: 10 mins | Serving: 4

Ingredients:
- Boneless chicken thighs – 17 oz (481 g)
- Brown sugar – 0.5 tsp (2.5 g)
- Flour – 2.6 oz (73 g)
- Tapioca flour – 1.4 oz (39 g)
- Buttermilk – 1 cup (235 ml)
- Egg – 1 (beaten)
- Garlic powder – 1 tsp (5 g)
- Garlic salt – 0.5 tsp (2.5 g)
- Onion powder – 0.5 tsp (2.5 g)
- Oregano – 0.25 tsp (1 g)
- Paprika – 0.5 tsp (2.5 g)
- Salt and pepper – to taste

Method:
1. Take a large bowl and add the hot sauce and buttermilk, mixing well
2. Take a plastic zip lock bag and add the tapioca flour, black pepper, and garlic salt, combining well. Turn the mixture out onto a large plate
3. Dip the thicken thighs into the buttermilk mixture, coating on all sides
4. Dip into the spice mixture, the egg, and finally the flour
5. Cook for 10 minutes at 190°C (370°F).

Nutrition per serving:

Calories – 305 | Fat - 7g | Carbs - 26g | Protein - 20g | Sugar – 4g | Fiber – 1g | Potassium - 55mg | Sodium – 360mg | Cholesterol – 75mg

7.15 Turkey Bites

Preparation Time: 5 mins |

Cooking Time: 12 mins | Serving: 4

Ingredients:
- Ground turkey – 17 oz (481 g)
- Breadcrumbs – 5 oz (141 g)
- Egg - 1
- Olive oil – 2 tbsp (30 ml)

Method:
1. Mix together the oil and breadcrumbs in a large bowl
2. Take the ground turkey and create small patties with your hands
3. Dip the patties into the egg, then the breadcrumb mixture
4. Place inside the air fryer
5. Repeat the same process with the remaining turkey mixture
6. Cook for 12 minutes at 190°C (370°F).

Nutrition per serving:

Calories – 213 | Fat - 7g | Carbs - 9g | Protein - 26g | Sugar – 3g | Fiber – 0.5g | Potassium - 50mg | Sodium – 150mg | Cholesterol – 70mg

8 PORK RECIPES

8.1 Pork Tenderloin in Dijon Mustard

Preparation Time: 35 mins |

Cooking Time: 30 mins | Serving: 2

Ingredients:
- Pork tenderloin – 1
- Soy sauce – 3 tbsp (45 ml)
- Garlic cloves – 2 (minced)
- Olive oil – 3 tbsp (45 ml)
- Brown sugar – 2 tbsp (30 g)
- Dijon mustard – 1 tbsp (15 g)
- Salt and pepper – to taste

Method:
1. Take a bowl and combine the ingredients, except for the pork
2. Pour the mixture into a zip lock bag and then add the pork
3. Close the top and make sure the pork is well covered
4. Place in the refrigerator for 30 minutes
5. Preheat your air fryer to 200°C (390°F)
6. Remove the pork from the bag and place it in the fryer
7. Cook for 25 minutes, turning halfway
8. Remove and rest for 5 minutes before slicing into pieces

Nutrition per serving:

Calories – 450 | Fat - 9g | Carbs - 14g | Protein - 40g | Sugar – 10g | Fiber – 0.4g | Potassium - 390mg | Sodium – 650mg | Cholesterol – 90mg

8.2 Breaded Pork Chops

Preparation Time: 5 mins |

Cooking Time: 10 mins | Serving: 2

Ingredients:
- Salt and pepper – to taste
- Paprika – 0.5 tsp (2.5 g)
- Thyme – 0.5 tsp (2.5 g)
- Onion powder - 0.5 tsp (2.5 g)
- Garlic powder – 0.5 tsp (2.5 g)
- Mayonnaise – 2 tbsp (30 g)
- Pork chops - 2
- Italian breadcrumbs – 8 oz (226 g)

Method:
1. Combine the breadcrumbs, garlic powder, paprika, salt and pepper, and thyme, and onion powder
2. Cover the pork chops with the mayonnaise making sure to cover both sides
3. Coat the meat with the seasoning mixture, making sure it is fully covered
4. Cook the pork chops in the fryer for 10 minutes at 200°C (390°F), turning over halfway

Nutrition per serving:

Calories – 300 | Fat - 9g | Carbs - 5g | Protein - 22g | Sugar – 1g | Fiber – 0.5g | Potassium - 300mg | Sodium – 400mg | Cholesterol – 70mg

8.3 Pork & Marinara Sub

Preparation Time: 5 mins |

Cooking Time: 15 mins | Serving: 2

Ingredients:
- Pork meatballs - 8
- Marinara sauce – 5 tbsp (75 ml)
- Grated cheese – 5 oz (141 g)
- Hotdog rolls - 2
- Dried oregano – 0.25 tsp (5 ml)

Method:
1. Place the meatballs in the air fryer and cook for around 10 minutes, turning halfway through
2. Coat the meatballs in the marinara sauce
3. Cover with the oregano
4. Take the bread roll and add the mixture inside
5. Top with the cheese
6. Place the meatball sub back in the air fryer and cook for 2 minutes at 200°C (390°F)

Nutrition per serving:

Calories – 390 | Fat - 6g | Carbs - 12g | Protein - 24g | Sugar – 1g | Fiber – 1.5g | Potassium - 290mg | Sodium – 480mg | Cholesterol – 55mg

8.4 BBQ Ribs

Preparation Time: 4 hours |

Cooking Time: 30 mins | Serving: 2

Ingredients:
- Five spice – 0.5 tsp (2.5 g)
- Sesame oil – 1 tsp (5 ml)
- Salt – 1 tsp (5 g)
- Black pepper – 1 tsp (5 g)
- Soy sauce – 1 tsp (5 g)
- Garlic cloves – 3
- Bbq sauce – 4 tbsp (60 ml)
- Honey – 1 tbsp (15 ml)
- Ribs – 17 oz (481 g)

Method:
1. Chop the ribs into small pieces and place them in a bowl
2. Add all the ingredients into the bowl and mix well
3. Marinate for 4 hours
4. Preheat the air fryer to 180°C (350°F)
5. Place the ribs into the air fryer and cook for 14 minutes
6. Coat the ribs in honey and cook for a further 16 minutes

Nutrition per serving:

Calories – 554 | Fat - 21g | Carbs - 19g | Protein - 62g | Sugar – 15g | Fiber – 0.6g | Potassium - 300mg | Sodium – 600mg | Cholesterol – 140mg

8.5 Pork Schnitzel

Preparation Time: 5 mins |

Cooking Time: 20 mins | Serving: 2

Ingredients:
- Pork steaks – 3 (cubes)
- Eggs - 2
- Flour – 6 oz - 1 1/4 cup (170 g)
- Breadcrumbs – 6 oz - 2 cup (170 g)
- Salt and pepper – to taste

Method:
1. Season the pork with salt and pepper
2. Coat the pork in the flour and then dip in the egg
3. Coat the pork in breadcrumbs
4. Place in the air fryer and cook at 180°C (350°F) for 20 minutes, turning halfway

Nutrition per serving:

Calories – 426 | Fat - 21g | Carbs - 22g | Protein - 38g | Sugar – 2g | Fiber – 1.2g | Potassium - 320mg | Sodium – 360mg | Cholesterol – 150mg

8.6 Fruity Balsamic Pork Chops

Preparation Time: 5 mins |

Cooking Time: 24 mins | Serving: 2

Ingredients:
- Pork chops - 4
- Eggs – 2
- Milk – 0.1 cup (23 ml)
- Breadcrumbs – 8 oz - 4 1/2 cup (481 g)
- Pecans – 8 oz (481 g) (chopped)
- Orange juice – 1 tbsp (15 ml)
- Balsamic vinegar – 0.1 cups (23 ml)
- Brown sugar – 2 tbsp (30 g)
- Raspberry jam – 2 tbsp (30 g)

Method:
1. Mix the eggs and milk together in a bowl
2. In another bowl mix the breadcrumbs and pecans
3. Coat the pork chops in flour, egg and then coat in the breadcrumbs
4. Place in the air fryer and cook for 12 minutes at 200°C (390°F), turning halfway
5. Put the remaining ingredients in a pan simmer for about 6 minutes
6. Serve the sauce with the pork chops.

Nutrition per serving:

Calories – 579 | Fat - 30g | Carbs - 20g | Protein - 38g | Sugar – 16g | Fiber – 2.5g | Potassium - 310mg | Sodium – 340mg | Cholesterol – 140mg

8.7 Chinese Spiced Pork

Preparation Time: 5 mins |

Cooking Time: 12 mins | Serving: 2

Ingredients:
- Pork – 2 (chunks)
- Eggs - 2
- Sesame oil – 1 tsp (5 ml)
- Cornstarch – 7 oz - 1 1/2 cup -(198 g)
- Salt – 0.25 tsp (1 g)
- Pepper – 0.5 tsp (2.5 g)
- Canola oil – 3 tbsp (45 ml)
- Chinese five spice – 1 tsp (5 ml)

Method:
1. Mix the corn starch, salt, pepper, and five spice together
2. Mix the eggs and sesame oil in another bowl
3. Dip the pork into the egg and then cover in the cornstarch mix
4. Place in the air fryer and cook at 180°C (350°F) for 11-12 minutes, shaking halfway through

Nutrition per serving:

Calories – 510 | Fat - 32g | Carbs - 19g | Protein - 35g | Sugar – 2g | Fiber – 0.6g | Potassium - 330mg | Sodium – 210mg | Cholesterol – 150mg

8.8 Pineapple Pork

Preparation Time: 5 mins |

Cooking Time: 17 mins | Serving: 2

Ingredients:
- Oil – 1 tsp (5 ml)
- Soy – 1 tbsp (15 ml)
- Brown sugar – 1 tbsp (15 g)
- Pepper – 0.5 tsp (2.5 g)
- Salt – 0.5 tsp (2.5 g)
- Ginger - 1
- Garlic - 1 clove (minced)
- Red pepper - 1 (sliced)
- Fresh coriander (chopped) –
10. 2.6 oz - 1 1/4cup (73 g)
- Pineapple – ½
- Pork loin – 15 oz (425 g) (cubed)

Method:
1. Add salt and pepper to the pork
2. Place all ingredients in the air fryer and cook for 17 minutes at 180°C (350°F).
3. Serve with coriander garnish

Nutrition per serving:

Calories – 256 | Fat - 10g | Carbs - 15g | Protein - 7g | Sugar – 2g | Fiber – 2.5g | Potassium - 300mg | Sodium – 320mg | Cholesterol – 55mg

8.9 Seasoned Belly Pork

Preparation Time: 5 mins |

Cooking Time: 15 mins | Serving: 4

Ingredients:
- Belly pork – 17 oz (481 g)
- Salt and pepper – to taste

Method:
1. Cut the pork into bite-size pieces and season with salt and pepper
2. Heat the air fryer to 200°C (390°F)
3. Cook for 15 minutes, until crisp

Nutrition per serving:

Calories – 332 | Fat - 24g | Carbs - 10g | Protein - 10g | Sugar – 2g | Fiber – 0g | Potassium - 350mg | Sodium – 240mg | Cholesterol – 70mg

8.10 Pork & Ginger Meatballs

Preparation Time: 5 mins |

Cooking Time: 10 mins | Serving: 4

Ingredients:
- Minced pork – 17 oz (481 g)
- Eggs - 2
- Breadcrumbs – 3.5 oz - 1 1/4 cup (99 g)
- Spring onions – 2 (diced)
- Garlic – 1 tsp (5 g)
- Chili flakes – 0.5 tsp (2.5 g)
- Sesame oil – 1 tsp (5 g)
- Soy sauce – 1 tsp (5 g)
- Salt and pepper - to taste

Method:
1. Mix all ingredients in a bowl
2. Form mixes into 1.5" sized meatballs
3. Place in the air fryer and cook at 200°C (390°F) for about 10 minutes

Nutrition per serving:

Calories – 486 | Fat - 20g | Carbs - 21g | Protein - 10g | Sugar – 1g | Fiber – 1g | Potassium - 210mg | Sodium – 380mg | Cholesterol – 90mg

9 BEEF RECIPES

9.1 Steak & Asparagus Cubes

Preparation Time: 1 hour |

Cooking Time: 5 mins | Serving: 2

Ingredients:
- Steak – 17 oz (481 g) (cubes)
- Tamari sauce – 0.3 oz (8.5 ml)
- Garlic cloves – 2 (crushed)
- Asparagus – 8 oz (99 g) (trimmed)
- Bell peppers – 3 large (sliced)
- Butter – 2 tbsp (30 g)
- Salt and pepper – to taste

Method:
1. Season the steak to your liking
2. Place the meat in a zip-top bag and add the Tamari and garlic, sealing the bag closed. Leave in the refrigerator for at least 1 hour
3. Remove the steaks from the bag and throw the marinade away
4. Place the peppers and sliced asparagus in the center of each steak piece
5. Roll the steak up and secure it in place
6. Transfer the meat parcels to the air fryer and cook for 5 minutes at 200°C (390°F)
7. Melt the butter in a saucepan, adding the juices from the air fryer, cooking until thickened
8. Pour the sauce over the steak

Nutrition per serving:

Calories – 486 | Fat - 21g | Carbs - 25g | Protein - 10g | Sugar – 1g | Fiber – 4g | Potassium - 310mg | Sodium – 420mg | Cholesterol – 85mg

9.2 Mexican Steak & Chips

Preparation Time: 5 mins |

Cooking Time: 9 mins | Serving: 2

Ingredients:
- Sirloin steak – 17 oz (481 g)
- French fries – 1 bag
- Grated cheese – 12 oz (340 g)
- Sour cream – 2 tbsp (30 g)
- Guacamole - 2 tbsp (30 g)
- Steak seasoning – 2 tbsp (30 ml)
- Salt and pepper – to taste

Method:
1. Place in the air fryer and cook for 4 minutes at 180°C (350°F)
2. Turnover and cooking for another 4 minutes
3. Remove and allow to rest
4. Add the French fries to the fryer and cook for 5 minutes, shaking regularly
5. Add the cheese
6. Cut the steak into pieces and add on top of the cheese
7. Cook for another 30 seconds, until the cheese is melted

Nutrition per serving:

Calories – 436 | Fat - 22g | Carbs - 22g | Protein - 9g | Sugar – 1g | Fiber – 3g | Potassium - 360mg | Sodium – 530mg | Cholesterol – 75mg

9.3 Beef Wellington

Preparation Time: 1 hour |

Cooking Time: 35 mins | Serving: 2

Ingredients:

- Shortcrust pastry – 17 oz (481 g)
- Beef fillet – 21 oz (588 g)
- Chicken pate – 10 oz (284 g)
- Egg - 1
- Salt and pepper – to taste

Method:

1. Season the beef and wrap in plastic wrap. Place in the refrigerator for 1 hour
2. Roll out the pastry and brush the egg over the edges
3. Spread the pate over the pastry
4. Remove the clingfilm from the beef and place it in the center of the pastry, sealing around the meat
5. Place in the air fryer and cook at 160°C (320°F) for 35 minutes

Nutrition per serving:

Calories – 256 | Fat - 9g | Carbs - 10g | Protein - 6g | Sugar – 2g | Fiber – 1g | Potassium - 380mg | Sodium – 420mg | Cholesterol – 90mg

9.4 Coconut Asian Beef

Preparation Time: 5 mins |

Cooking Time: 25 mins | Serving: 2

Ingredients:

- Coconut oil – 1 tbsp (15 g)
- Steak – 21 oz (588 g) (slices)
- Red peppers – 2 (sliced)
- Liquid aminos – 0.4 cups (94 ml)
- Water – 0.4 cups (94 ml)
- Brown sugar – 3.5 oz - 1/2 cup (99 g)
- Ground ginger – 0.5 tsp (2.5 g)
- Minced garlic – 0.5 tbsp (7.5 g)
- Red pepper flakes – 1 tsp (5 g)
- Salt and pepper – to taste

Method:

1. In a pan, melt the coconut oil and sauté the peppers until tender.
2. In another pan add the pepper flakes, garlic, ginger, brown sugar and aminos. Mix and bring to the boil, simmering for 10 mins
3. Place the steak in the air fryer for 10 minutes at 180°C (350°F)
4. Turnover and cook for a further 5 minutes
5. Combine the beef with the peppers and sauce

Nutrition per serving:

Calories – 356 | Fat - 33g | Carbs - 15g | Protein - 10g | Sugar – 12g | Fiber – 1.5g | Potassium - 400mg | Sodium – 620mg | Cholesterol – 60mg

9.5 Beef Fried Rice

Preparation Time: 5 mins |

Cooking Time: 10 mins | Serving: 2

Ingredients:
- Rice – 14 oz - 2 cup (396 g) (cooked)
- vegetable oil – 1 tbsp (15 ml)
- Beef strips -8 oz (99 g) (pre-cooked)
- Peas – 8 oz (99 g)
- Sesame oil – 1 tbsp (15 g)
- Onion - 1 (diced)
- Egg - 1
- Garlic powder – 2 tsp (30 g)
- Salt and pepper – to taste

Method:
1. Season the beef with salt, pepper, and garlic powder, cook in a pan until about ¾ done
2. Mix the rice with peas carrots and vegetable oil, add the beef, and mix
3. Add to the air fryer and cook for about 10 minutes at 190°C (370°F)
4. Add the egg and cook

Nutrition per serving:

Calories – 325 | Fat - 46g | Carbs - 14g | Protein - 7g | Sugar – 1g | Fiber – 3g | Potassium - 330mg | Sodium – 280mg | Cholesterol – 50mg

9.6 Feta Hamburgers

Preparation Time: 5 mins |

Cooking Time: 15 mins | Serving: 2

Ingredients:
- 14 oz (396 g) minced beef
- 8 oz (224 g) feta, crumbled
- 0.8 oz (22 g) green olives, chopped
- 0.5 tsp (2.5 g) garlic powder
- 0.5 onion, chopped
- 2 tbsp (30 ml) Worcestershire sauce
- 0.5 tsp (2.5 ml) steak seasoning
- Salt and pepper

Method:
1. Mix all the ingredients in a bowl
2. Divide the mix into four and shape into patties
3. Place in the air fryer and cook at 200°C (390°F) for about 15 minutes

Nutrition per serving:

Calories – 334 | Fat - 22g | Carbs - 10g | Protein - 9g | Sugar – 1g | Fiber – 1g | Potassium - 310mg | Sodium – 540mg | Cholesterol – 70mg

9.7 Stuffed Peppers with Beef

Preparation Time: 5 mins |

Cooking Time: 11 mins | Serving: 2

Ingredients:
- Beef – 17 oz (481 g) (minced)
- Bell peppers - 4
- Rice – 2.5 oz (70 g) (cooked)
- Onion – ½ (chopped)
- Garlic clove – 1 (minced)
- Tomato sauce – 5 tbsp (75 ml)
- Cheese – 3.5 oz (99 g) (grated)
- Worcestershire sauce – 2 tsp (10 ml)
- Garlic powder – 1 tsp (5 g)
- Chili powder – 0.5 tsp (2.5 g)
- Dried basil – 1 tsp (5 g)
- Salt and pepper – to taste

Method:
1. Cook the onions, minced beef, garlic, and all the seasonings until the meat is browned
2. Remove from the heat and add Worcestershire sauce, rice, half the cheese, and most of the tomato sauce. Mix well
3. Stuff the peppers with the mixture and place in the air fryer
4. Cook at 200°C (390°F) for 11 minutes
5. Toward the end of the cooking time, add the rest of the tomato sauce and cheese

Nutrition per serving:

Calories – 332 | Fat - 4g | Carbs – 9g | Protein - 5g | Sugar – 2g | Fiber – 4g | Potassium - 310mg | Sodium – 290mg | Cholesterol – 65mg

9.8 Paprika Steak and Mushrooms

Preparation Time: 4 hours |

Cooking Time: 10 mins | Serving: 2

Ingredients:
- Paprika – 1 tsp (5 g)
- Parsley flakes – 1 tsp (5 g)
- Olive oil -1 tbsp (15 ml)
- Worcestershire sauce – 3 tbsp (45 ml)
- Button mushrooms – 10 oz (284 g)
- Sirloin steak – 17 oz (481 g) (cubes)
- Chili flakes – 1 tsp (5 g) (crushed)

Method:
1. Combine all Ingredients in a bowl, cover, and chill for at least 4 hours
2. Place the steak and mushrooms in the air fryer and cook for 5 minutes at 200°C (390°F)
3. Shake and cook for a further 5 minutes

Nutrition per serving:

Calories – 190 | Fat - 4g | Carbs – 9g | Protein - 5g | Sugar – 2g | Fiber – 2.5g | Potassium - 210mg | Sodium – 320mg | Cholesterol – 70mg

9.9 Beef Enchiladas

Preparation Time: 5 mins |

Cooking Time: 10 mins | Serving: 4

Ingredients:
- Beef – 17 oz (481 g) (minced)
- Flour tortillas - 8
- Taco – 1 packet (seasoning)
- Cheese – 10 oz (284 g) (grated)
- Sour cream – 5 oz (142 g)
- Black beans – 1 can
- Tomatoes – 1 can (chopped)
- Chilies – 1 can
- Red enchilada sauce – 1 can
- Coriander, chopped – 10 oz (284 g)

Method:
1. Brown the beef and add the taco seasoning
2. Add the beef, beans, tomatoes, and chilies to the tortillas
3. Line the air fryer with foil and put the tortillas in
4. Pour the enchilada sauce over the top and sprinkle with cheese
5. Cook at 200°C (390°F) for five minutes

Nutrition per serving:

Calories – 546 | Fat - 20g | Carbs - 26g | Protein - 5g | Sugar – 2g | Fiber – 6g | Potassium - 390mg | Sodium – 600mg | Cholesterol – 50mg

9.10 Spicy Steak Wraps

Preparation Time: 4 hours |

Cooking Time: 14 mins | Serving: 4

Ingredients:
- Steak – 17 oz (481 g) (sliced)
- Pineapple juice – 0.8 oz (22.6 g)
- Onion – 1 (sliced) and
- Pepper - 1(sliced)
- Lime juice – 2 tbsp (30 ml)
- Olive oil – 1 tbsp (15 ml)
- Soy sauce – 1 tbsp (15 ml)
- Minced garlic- 1 tbsp (15 g)
- Chili powder – 0.5 tbsp (7.5 g)
- Paprika – ½ tsp (2.5 g)
- Cumin – ½ tsp (2.5 g)
- Salt and pepper – to taste

Method:
1. Mix the pineapple juice, lime juice, olive oil, soy sauce, garlic, cumin chili powder, and paprika. Pour over the steak and marinate for 4 hours
2. Add the peppers and onions inside the air fryer, season with salt and pepper
3. Cook at 200°C (390°F) for 10 minutes, add the steak and cook for another 7 minutes
4. Place the mixture inside the tortillas and place inside the air fryer
5. Cook for 4 minutes at 180°C (350°F)
6. Turnover and cook for another 3 minutes

Nutrition per serving:

Calories – 220 | Fat - 10g | Carbs - 9g | Protein - 5g | Sugar – 1g | Fiber – 2g | Potassium - 350mg | Sodium – 420mg | Cholesterol – 50mg

10 LAMB RECIPES

10.1 Classic Lamb Patties

Preparation Time: 5 mins |

Cooking Time: 18 mins | Serving: 2

Ingredients:
- Minced lamb – 21 oz (595 g)
- Garlic puree – 2 tsp (10 ml)
- Harissa paste – 1 tsp (5 g)
- Salt and pepper – to taste

Method:
1. Place all the ingredients in a bowl and mix well
2. Form into patties
3. Place in the air fryer and cook at 180°C (350°F) for 18 minutes

Nutrition per serving:

Calories – 478 | Fat - 19g | Carbs - 20g | Protein - 10g | Sugar – 2g | Fiber – <1g | Potassium - 300mg | Sodium – 230mg | Cholesterol – 85mg

10.2 Lamb & Worcestershire Sauce Peppers

Preparation Time: 5 mins |

Cooking Time: 11 mins | Serving: 2

Ingredients:
- Bell peppers - 4
- Lamb – 17 oz (481 g) (minced)
- Rice – 2.6 oz (73 g) (cooked)
- Onion – ½ (chopped)
- garlic clove, minced – 1 (minced)
- tomato sauce – 5 tbsp (75 ml)
- Worcestershire sauce – 2 tsp (10 g)
- grated cheese – 3.5 oz (99 g)
- garlic powder – 1 tsp (5 g)
- chili powder – 0.5 tsp (2.5 g)
- dried basil – 1 tsp (5 g)
- Salt and pepper – to taste

Method:
1. Cook the onions, minced lamb, garlic, and seasonings until the meat is browned
2. Remove from the heat and add Worcestershire sauce, rice, cheese, and tomato sauce
3. Place the mixture inside the peppers and place in the air fryer
4. Cook at 200°C (390°F) for about 11 minutes

Nutrition per serving:

Calories – 332 | Fat - 10g | Carbs - 12g | Protein - 10g | Sugar – 2g | Fiber – 3g | Potassium - 350mg | Sodium – 480mg | Cholesterol – 75mg

10.3 Lamb & Jalapeño Empanadas

Preparation Time: 5 mins |

Cooking Time: 12 mins | Serving: 4

Ingredients:
- Olive oil – 2 tsp (10 ml)
- Shortcrust pastry – 2 packets
- Lamb – 17 oz (481 g) (minced)
- Egg – 1 (beaten)
- Onion – 1 (chopped)
- Clove garlic – 1 (chopped)
- Jalapeño – 2 tbsp (30 g) (chopped)
- Cheddar cheese – 3.5 oz (99 g) (grated)
- Salt and pepper – to taste

Method:
1. Heat the oil in a pan and fry the onion and garlic until soft
2. Add the meat and jalapeño, season with salt and pepper, and cook until browned
3. Allow the meat to cool
4. Roll out dough as thin as possible and cut into circles
5. Add some of the mixture and top with cheese
6. Fold over the edges and brush with the beaten egg
7. Cook for about 12 minutes at 180°C (350°F)

Nutrition per serving:

Calories – 300 | Fat - 10g | Carbs - 16g | Protein - 10g | Sugar – 1g | Fiber – 1.5g | Potassium - 390mg | Sodium – 260mg | Cholesterol – 80mg

10.4 Lamb Kebabs

Preparation Time: 35 mins |

Cooking Time: 10 mins | Serving: 4

Ingredients:
- Lamb – 17 oz (481 g) (cubed)
- Sour cream – 0.8 oz (22 g)
- Bell pepper – 1 (chunks)
- Onion – ½ (chunks)
- Soy sauce – 2 tbsp (30 ml)
- Metal skewers - 8

Method:
1. Mix the sour cream and soy sauce in a bowl
2. Add the lamb and marinate for at least 30 minutes
3. Thread beef, bell peppers, and onion onto skewers
4. Cook in the air fryer at 200°C (390°F) for 10 minutes, turning halfway

Nutrition per serving:

Calories – 290 | Fat - 4g | Carbs - 9g | Protein - 5g | Sugar – 2g | Fiber – 1.5g | Potassium - 310mg | Sodium – 500mg | Cholesterol – 70mg

10.5 Lamb & Ginger Burgers

Preparation Time: 30 mins |

Cooking Time: 10 mins | Serving: 4

Ingredients:
- Dressings:
11. Olive oil – 1 tbsp (15 ml)
12. Sugar – 2 tsp (10 g)
13. Soy – 1 tbsp (15 g)
- Garlic – 2 tsp (10 g) (minced)
- Onion – 1 (chopped)
- Minced lamb – 17 oz (481 g)

Method:
1. Combine all ingredients and rest for at least 30 minutes in the refrigerator
2. Divide the meat into four and form into patties
3. Place in the air fryer and cook at 190°C (370°F) for 10 minutes

Nutrition per serving:
Calories – 392 | Fat - 20g | Carbs - 15g | Protein - 7g | Sugar – 1g | Fiber – 1g | Potassium - 390mg | Sodium – 250mg | Cholesterol – 80mg

10.6 Cheesy Lamb Balls

Preparation Time: 5 mins |

Cooking Time: 14 mins | Serving: 2

Ingredients:
- Taco seasoning - 2 tbsp (30 ml)
- Water – 1 tbsp (15 ml)
- Ground lamb – 17 oz (481 g)
- Green chillis – 1 can (chopped)
- Egg white – 1 (beaten)
- Cheddar cheese – 16 (small cubes)
- Tortilla chips – 10 oz (284 g) (crushed)

Method:
1. Combine the lamb with the green chilies and taco seasoning
2. Create small meatballs out of the mixture
3. Place a cube of cheese in the middle of each meatball and close around the edges
4. Dip every meatball into the egg white and then the crushed chips
5. Place the balls into the air fryer and cook at 190°C (370°F) for 14 minutes, turning halfway

Nutrition per serving:
Calories – 200 | Fat - 9g | Carbs - 15g | Protein - 9g | Sugar – 1g | Fiber – 2g | Potassium - 310mg | Sodium – 500mg | Cholesterol – 90mg

10.7 Spicy Lamb Meatloaf

Preparation Time: 5 mins |

Cooking Time: 15 mins | Serving: 2

Ingredients:
- Dressings:
  14. Salt and pepper – to taste
  15. Cinnamon – 0.5 tsp (2.5 g)
  16. Turmeric – 1 tsp (5 g)
  17. Cayenne – 1 tsp (5 g)
  18. Garam masala – 2 tsp (10 g)
- Minced garlic – 1 tbsp (15 g)
- Cardamom pod – to taste
- Ginger – to taste (minced)
- Coriander – 7 oz (20 g) (sliced)
- Onion -1 (diced)
- Eggs - 2
- Minced lamb – 17 oz (481 g)

Method:
1. Place all the Ingredients in a large bowl and combine
2. Form a loaf shape with the mixture and place in the air fryer
3. Cook for 15 minutes at 190°C (370°F)
4. Slice before serving

Nutrition per serving:

Calories – 290 | Fat - 4g | Carbs - 9g | Protein - 5g | Sugar – 2g | Fiber – 1.5g | Potassium - 290mg | Sodium – 150mg | Cholesterol – 270mg

10.8 Mushroom & Onion "Pasties"

Preparation Time: 30 mins |

Cooking Time: 15 mins | Serving: 2

Ingredients:
- Minced lamb – 10 oz (284 g)
- Olive oil – 1 tbsp (15 ml)
- Egg – 1
- Gyoza wrappers - 8
- Onion – 1 (chopped)
- Mushrooms – 5 oz (142 g) (chopped)
- Tomatoes – 4 (chopped)
- Green olives - 6
- Cinnamon – 0.5 tsp (2.5 g)
- Garlic – 2 tsp (10 g) (chopped)
- Paprika – 0.25 tsp (1 g)
- Cumin – 0.25 tsp (1 g)

Method:
1. Heat the oil in a pan. Add the onion and minced lamb. Cook until browned
2. Add the mushrooms and cook for 6 minutes more
3. Add garlic, olives, paprika, cumin, and cinnamon, and cook for about 3 minutes
4. Stir in tomatoes and cook for 1 minute. Place the mixture to one side for 20 minutes
5. Place a spoonful of the mixture into each wrapper
6. Brush the edges with egg and fold over to seal
7. Place in the air fryer and cook at 200°C (390°F) for 7 minutes

Nutrition per serving:

Calories – 353 | Fat - 19g | Carbs - 20g | Protein - 10g | Sugar – 2g | Fiber – 3g | Potassium - 320mg | Sodium – 400mg | Cholesterol – 175mg

10.9 Lasagna Taco Bake

Preparation Time: 5 mins |

Cooking Time: 8 mins | Serving: 2

Ingredients:
- Ground lamb – 15 oz (425 g)
- Olive oil – 2 tbsp (30 ml)
- Flour tortillas - 2
- Onion -1 (chopped)
- Garlic – 1 tbsp (15 g) (minced)
- Grated cheese – 8 oz (226 g)
- Tomato sauce – 3.8 oz (107 g)
- Cumin – 1 tsp (5 g)
- Oregano – 1 tsp (5 g)

Method:
1. Cook the onions with the oil in a frying pan, until soft
2. Add the lamb and garlic and cook until the meat has browned
3. Add the tomato sauce, cumin, and oregano and cook for 2 minutes
4. Place one tortilla on the bottom of your air fryer basket
5. Add a meat layer, followed by cheese, and continue until you have no ingredients left
6. Top with the remaining tortillas
7. Cook at 200°C (370°F) for 8 minutes

Nutrition per serving:

Calories – 390 | Fat - 20g | Carbs - 25g | Protein - 10g | Sugar – 2g | Fiber – 2.5g | Potassium - 370mg | Sodium – 500mg | Cholesterol – 115mg

10.10 Lamb & Parsley Roll

Preparation Time: 5 mins |

Cooking Time: 15 mins | Serving: 2

Ingredients:
- Olive oil – 2 tbsp (30 ml)
- Lamb – 14 oz (396 g)
- Onion – 1 (sliced)
- Dijon mustard – 4 tbsp (60 g)
- bacon – 4 slices (chopped)
- Sour cream – 4 tbsp (60 g)
- Tomato pastes -1 tbsp (15 g)
- Parsley (chopped) – 1 tsp (5 g)

Method:
1. Season the onions and cook in the air fryer at 200°C (390°F) for 5 minutes
2. Put half the onions in a bowl and mix with sour cream, 2 tsp parsley, and tomato paste
3. Spread the mustard onto the lamb, followed by the onions and the bacon pieces
4. Roll the lamb up and cook in the air fryer for 10 minutes

Nutrition per serving:

Calories – 440 | Fat - 20g | Carbs - 21g | Protein - 9g | Sugar – 1g | Fiber – 1.5g | Potassium - 360mg | Sodium – 600mg | Cholesterol – 125mg

11 DESSERT RECIPES

11.1 Vanilla Biscuits

Preparation Time: 5 mins |
Cooking Time: 15 mins | Serving: 6

Ingredients:
- Flour – 7 oz (200 g)
- Sugar – 3.5 oz (100 g)
- Butter – 3.5 oz (100 g)
- Egg - 1
- Vanilla essence -1 tsp (5 g)

Method:
1. Rub together the flour, butter, and sugar
2. Add the egg and vanilla to form a dough
3. Split the dough into 6 and form it into balls
4. Place in the air fryer cook at 190°C (370°F) for 15 minutes

Nutrition per serving:

Calories – 226 | Fat - 10g | Carbs - 15g | Protein - 2g | Sugar – 2g | Fiber – 0.5g | Potassium - 120mg | Sodium – 100mg | Cholesterol – 35mg

11.2 Orange Cocoa Dip

Preparation Time: 5 mins |
Cooking Time: 12 mins | Serving: 4

Ingredients:
- Flour – 2 tbsp (30 g)
- Eggs - 2
- Caster sugar – 4 tbsp (60 g)
- Dark chocolate – 4 oz (113 g)
- Orange juice – 4 oz (113 g)
- Ramekin dishes – 4 (greased)

Method:
1. Place the chocolate and butter in a glass dish and melt over a pan of hot water, stir until combined
2. Beat the eggs and sugar together until pale and fluffy
3. Add the orange juice and egg mix to the chocolate and combine
4. Stir in the flour until fully mixed together
5. Transfer the mixture into your ramekins
6. Place in the air fryer and cook at 190°C (370°F) for 12 minutes
7. Cool before consumption

Nutrition per serving:

Calories – 400 | Fat - 19g | Carbs - 17g | Protein - 4g | Sugar – 2g | Fiber – 1g | Potassium - 170mg | Sodium – 15mg | Cholesterol – 53mg

11.3 Delicious Profiteroles

Preparation Time: 5 mins |

Cooking Time: 10 mins | Serving: 4

Ingredients:
- Butter – 3.5 oz (99 g)
- Icing sugar – 2 tsp (10 g)
- Plain flour – 7 oz (198 g)
- Butter – 1.7 oz (48 g)
- Eggs - 6
- Water - 1.2 cups (280 ml)
- Vanilla extract – 2 tsp (10 ml)
- Whipped cream – 1.2 cups (280 ml)
- milk chocolate - 3.5 oz (100 g)
- Whipped cream – 2 tbsp

Method:
1. Place the butter and water in a pan over a medium heat and bring to the boil
2. Remove from the heat and stir in the flour to create a dough
3. Mix in the eggs and stir until mixture is smooth
4. Create the shapes of profiteroles with all the dough and place in the air fryer
5. Cook at 190°C (370°F) for 10 minutes
6. Meanwhile, combine the whipped cream, vanilla extract, and the icing sugar
7. Separately, melt the butter, and chocolate
8. Pipe the filling into the profiteroles and top with the chocolate

Nutrition per serving:
Calories – 390 | Fat - 27g | Carbs - 21g | Protein - 5g | Sugar – 2g | Fiber – 1g | Potassium - 200mg | Sodium – 100mg | Cholesterol – 95mg

11.4 Cherry Parcels

Preparation Time: 5 mins |

Cooking Time: 10 mins | Serving: 6

Ingredients:
- Shortcrust pastry – 10 oz (284 g) (cookie shapes)
- Cherry pie filling – 2.6 oz (73 g)
- Milk – 0.5 tsp (2.5 ml)
- Icing sugar – 3 tbsp (45 g)

Method:
1. Take your cookie pieces and add an equal amount of cherry filling in the middle of each
2. Fold over and use a fork to seal the edges
3. Cook in the air fryer at 190°C (370°F) for 10 minutes
4. Mix together the icing sugar and milk
5. Drizzle the mixture over the parcels once cooled

Nutrition per serving:
Calories – 290 | Fat - 4g | Carbs - 9g | Protein - 5g | Sugar – 2g | Fiber – 0.7g | Potassium - 200mg | Sodium – 60mg | Cholesterol – 5mg

11.5 Classic Creamy Cheesecake

Preparation Time: 6 hours |

Cooking Time: 45 mins | Serving: 8

Ingredients:
- Flour – 7 oz (198 g)
- Quark – 0.2 cups (47 g)
- Eggs - 3
- Cream cheese – 26 oz (737 g)
- Sugar – 7 oz (198 g)
- Brown sugar – 3.5 oz (99 g)
- Butter – 3.5 oz (99 g)
- Melted butter – 1.7 oz (48 ml)
- Vanilla essence – 1 tbsp (15 ml)
- Springform tin – 1 (greased)

Method:
1. Combine the flour, sugar, and 100g butter
2. Create rough biscuits and place them in the air fryer. Cook for 15 minutes at 370°F (190°C)
3. Once cooked, use a rolling pin to break the biscuits and combine with the melted butter
4. Press the mixture into the bottom of the tin
5. Combine the cream cheese and sugar, add the eggs and vanilla, and combine until smooth. Mix in the quark
6. Pour the cheesecake batter into the pan
7. Cook for 30 minutes at 190°C (370°F) and allow to cool for half an hour
8. Refrigerate for 6 hours

Nutrition per serving:

Calories – 831 | Fat - 30g | Carbs - 24g | Protein - 10g | Sugar – 2g | Fiber – 0.7g | Potassium - 200mg | Sodium – 220mg | Cholesterol – 140mg

11.6 Classic Apple Pie

Preparation Time: 5 mins |

Cooking Time: 30 mins | Serving: 6

Ingredients:
- Ready-made pastry – 1 packet
- Apple – 1 (chopped)
- Lemon juice – 2 tsp (10 ml)
- Egg - 1
- Sugar – 1 tbsp (15 g)
- Cinnamon -1 tsp (5 g)
- Sugar- 1 tbsp (15 g)
- Vanilla extract – 0.5 tsp (2.5 g)
- Butter – 1 tbsp (15 g)

Method:
1. Line a baking tin with pastry
2. Mix the apple, lemon juice, cinnamon, sugar, and vanilla in a bowl
3. Pour the apple mix into the tin with the pastry, top with chunks of butter
4. Cover with a second piece of pastry. Pierce slits in the top
5. Brush the pastry with the egg and sprinkle with sugar
6. Place in the air fryer and cook for 30 minutes at 190°C (370°F)

Nutrition per serving:

Calories – 486 | Fat - 19g | Carbs - 25g | Protein - 9g | Sugar – 2g | Fiber – 1g | Potassium - 250mg | Sodium – 160mg | Cholesterol – 45mg

11.7 Chocolate Soufflé

Preparation Time: 5 mins |

Cooking Time: 25 mins | Serving: 2

Ingredients:
- Milk chocolate – 5 oz (142 g) (chopped)
- Butter – 3 oz (85 g)
- Eggs – 2 (separated)
- Sugar – 3 tbsp (45 g)
- Vanilla extract – 0.5 tsp (2.5g)
- Flour – 2 tbsp (30 g)
- Ramekins – 2 (greased)

Method:
1. Melt the chocolate and butter together
2. Separately, beat together the egg yolks, sugar, and vanilla
3. Drizzle in the chocolate mix, add the flour, and combine
4. Whisk the egg whites to soft peaks, gently fold into the chocolate mix a little at a time
5. Add the mix to ramekins and place in the air fryer
6. Cook for about 14 minutes at 180°C (350°F)

Nutrition per serving:

Calories – 486 | Fat - 19g | Carbs - 20g | Protein - 9g | Sugar – 2g | Fiber – 2g | Potassium - 200mg | Sodium – 150mg | Cholesterol – 120mg

11.8 Classic Chocolate Cake

Preparation Time: 5 mins |

Cooking Time: 25 mins | Serving: 8

Ingredients:
- Flour – 7 oz (198 g)
- Cocoa powder – 0.8 oz (22 g)
- Sugar – 5 oz (142 g)
- Eggs - 3
- Sour cream – 0.3 cups (70 g)
- Vanilla extract – 2 tsp (10 ml)
- Baking powder – 1 tsp (5 g)
- Baking soda – 0.5 tsp (2.5 g)

Method:
1. Mix all the ingredients together in a bowl and transfer to a baking tin
2. Place into the air fryer and cook for 25 minutes at 180°C (350°F)

Nutrition per serving:

Calories – 573 | Fat - 30g | Carbs – 35g | Protein - 5g | Sugar – 2g | Fiber – 1.5g | Potassium - 180mg | Sodium – 200mg | Cholesterol – 55mg

11.9 Honey & Apple Pasties

Preparation Time: 5 mins |

Cooking Time: 18 mins | Serving: 12

Ingredients:
- Water – 1 tsp (5 ml)
- Cornstarch – 2 tsp (10 g)
- Nutmeg – 1 tsp (5 g)
- Cinnamon – 1 tsp (5 g)
- Vanilla extract – 1 tsp (5 g)
- Honey – 2 tbsp (30 ml)
- Apples – 2 (diced)
- Empanada wrappers - 12

Method:
1. Combine the apples, cinnamon, honey, vanilla, and nutmeg in a pan and cook for 2-3 minutes
2. Mix the cornstarch and water add to the pan and cook for 30 seconds
3. Add the apple mix to each of the empanada wraps
4. Roll the wrap in half, pinch along the edges, and seal
5. Cook for 8 minutes at 200°C (390°F)
6. Turnover and cook for another 10 minutes

Nutrition per serving:

Calories – 190 | Fat - 4g | Carbs - 9g | Protein - 5g | Sugar – 2g | Fiber – 0.8g | Potassium - 210mg | Sodium – 110mg | Cholesterol – 0mg

11.10 Banana & Walnut Bread

Preparation Time: 10 mins |

Cooking Time: 40 mins | Serving: 8

Ingredients:
- All-purpose flour – 1 ¾ cups (220 g)
- Bananas – 3 ripe (mashed)
- Walnuts – 1/2 cup (60 g) (chopped)
- Eggs - 2 large
- Granulated sugar – 3/4 cup (150 g)
- Ground cinnamon – 1 tsp (2.6 g)
- Salt – 1/4 tsp (1.5 g)
- Baking soda – 1 tsp (4 g)
- Plain Greek yogurt – 1/2 cup (120 g)
- Vegetable oil – 1/3 cup (80 ml)
- Vanilla extract – 1 tsp (5 ml)
- Air fryer-safe baking pan
- Cooking spray or butter for greasing the cake pan

Method:
1. Preheat your air fryer to 320°F (160°C). Mix flour, cinnamon, salt, and baking soda in one bowl.
2. In another, combine mashed bananas, eggs, sugar, yogurt, oil, and vanilla extract. Gently mix dry ingredients into the wet mix. Fold in walnuts.
3. Grease an air fryer-safe pan and pour the batter in. Cook in the air fryer for 35-40 minutes or until a toothpick comes out clean.
4. Let it cool in the pan for 10 minutes, then transfer to a wire rack.
5. Enjoy delicious, moist banana bread without turning on your oven!

Nutrition per serving:

Calories – 326 | Fat - 15g | Carbs - 43g | Protein - 6g | Sugar - 23g | Fiber - 3g | Potassium - 276mg | Sodium – 300mg | Cholesterol – 46mg

12 SNACK & APPETIZER RECIPES

12.1 Cheesy Garlic Bread

Preparation Time: 5 mins |

Cooking Time: 10 mins | Serving: 2

Ingredients:
- Egg - 1
- Grated cheese – 10 oz (284 g)
- garlic powder – 0.5 tsp (2.5 g)

Method:
1. Combine the ingredients and create round shapes on a piece of parchment paper
2. Place in the air fryer and cook for 10 minutes at 180°C (370°F)

Nutrition per serving:

Calories – 225 | Fat - 15g | Carbs - 19g | Protein - 3g | Sugar – 1g | Fiber – 0.2g | Potassium - 210mg | Sodium – 600mg | Cholesterol – 92.5mg

12.2 Chicken & Bacon BBQ Bites

Preparation Time: 5 mins |

Cooking Time: 10 mins | Serving: 6

Ingredients:
- 2 chicken breasts, cut into strips
- brown sugar - 2 tbsp (30 g)
- BBQ sauce - 0.8 oz (22.6 ml)
- bacon, cut into long pieces - 7 slices

Method:
1. Wrap two strips of the bacon around each piece of chicken
2. Brush the tops with the BBQ sauce and add some brown sugar to each
3. Cook for 5 minutes at 200°C (390°F), turn and cook for a further 5 minutes

Nutrition per serving:

Calories – 250 | Fat - 4g | Carbs - 9g | Protein - 5g | Sugar - 2g | Fiber - 0.3g | Potassium - 210mg | Sodium – 650mg | Cholesterol – 60mg

12.3 Onion Bhajis

Preparation Time: 12 mins |

Cooking Time: 12 mins | Serving: 8

Ingredients:
- Onion – 1 (sliced)
- Red onion – 1 (sliced)
- Jalapeño pepper – 1 (minced)
- Chickpea flour – 5 oz (142 g)
- Water – 4 tbsp (60ml)
- Garlic – 1 clove (minced)
- Coriander – 1 tsp (5 g)
- Cumin - 0.5 tsp (2.5 g)
- Turmeric – 1 tsp (5 g)
- Salt and pepper – to taste

Method:
1. Combine all ingredients in a large bowl and create round balls using your hands
2. Cook for 6 minutes on each side at 200°C (390°F)

Nutrition per serving:

Calories – 290 | Fat - 10g | Carbs - 9g | Protein - 10g | Sugar – 1g | Fiber – 2.2g | Potassium - 190mg | Sodium – 320mg | Cholesterol – 0mg

12.4 Spicy Pork Bites

Preparation Time: 30 mins |

Cooking Time: 15 mins | Serving: 2

Ingredients:
- Pork mince – 14 oz (396 g)
- Thai curry paste – 2 tbsp (30 g)
- Worcester sauce – 1 tbsp (15 ml)
- Lime – 1 (juice and zest)
- Onion - 1 (chopped finely)
- Soy sauce – 1 tbsp (15 g)
- Garlic pastes – 1 tsp (5g)
- Coriander – 1 tsp (5 g)
- Mixed spice – 1 tsp (5 g)
- Salt and pepper – to taste

Method:
1. Take a large bowl and combine all ingredients to create a smooth mixture
2. Use your hands to create small balls
3. Refrigerate for half an hour
4. Cook in the air fryer for 15 minutes, at 180°C (350°F)

Nutrition per serving:

Calories – 292 | Fat - 4g | Carbs - 9g | Protein - 5g | Sugar - 2g | Fiber - 1g | Potassium - 210mg | Sodium – 680mg | Cholesterol – 80mg

12.5 Stringy Mozzarella Sticks

Preparation Time: 5 mins |

Cooking Time: 12 mins | Serving: 6

Ingredients:

Dressings:
- Salt and pepper – to taste
- Basil – 0.5 tsp (2.5 g)
- Oregano – 0.25 tsp (1 g)
- Onion powder – 0.5 tsp (2.5 g)
- Salt – 0.5 tsp (2.5 g)
- Garlic powder – 1 tsp (5 g)
- Parsley – 0.5 tsp (2.5 g)
- Flour - 1.7 oz (48 g)
- Cornmeal – 1 tbsp (15 g)
- Breadcrumbs – 3.5 oz (99 g)
- Cornstarch – 5 tbsp (75 g)
- Water – 0.25 cups (59 ml)
- Mozzarella cheese – 7 (cut into strips)

Method:
1. Combine the water, cornmeal, cornstarch flour, garlic powder, and salt
2. Separately, combine the breadcrumbs, pepper, basil parsley, onion powder, and oregano
3. Dip the mozzarella sticks in the batter then cover in the breadcrumbs
4. Cook for 6 minutes at 200°C (390°F)
5. Turn and cook for another 6 minutes

Nutrition per serving:

Calories – 686 | Fat - 25g | Carbs - 20g | Protein - 8g | Sugar – 1g | Fiber – 1.5g | Potassium - 2180mg | Sodium – 480mg | Cholesterol – 25mg

12.6 Picnic Scotch Eggs

Preparation Time: 5 mins |

Cooking Time: 12 mins | Serving: 6

Ingredients:
- Pork sausage – 10 oz (284 g)
- Eggs - 2
- Boiled eggs - 6
- Flour – 1.7 oz (48 g)
- Breadcrumbs – 7 oz (198 g)

Method:
1. Divide the mashed sausage into six equal portions
2. Place an egg in the middle of each portion and close all the edges using your hands
3. Dip first in the flour, the egg, and the breadcrumbs
4. Cook in the air fryer at 200°C (390°F) for 12 minutes

Nutrition per serving:

Calories – 407 | Fat - 10g | Carbs - 17g | Protein - 9g | Sugar - 1g | Fiber - 1g | Potassium - 150mg | Sodium – 520mg | Cholesterol – 185mg

12.7 Cheesy Carrot Mushrooms

Preparation Time: 5 mins |

Cooking Time: 8 mins | Serving: 6

Ingredients:

- Mushrooms - 24
- Bacon – 2 slices (chopped)
- Cheese – 7 oz (198 g) (grated)
- Red pepper – 1 (sliced)
- Onion – 1 (diced)
- Carrot – 1 (diced)
- Sour cream – 3.5 oz (99 g)

Method:

1. Combine the pepper, carrot, onion, and bacon in a pan and cook until soft, for around 5 minutes
2. Add the sour cream and cheese and combine until smooth
3. Stuff the mushrooms with the mixture and place in the air fryer
4. Cook at 180°C (350°F) for 8 minutes

Nutrition per serving:

Calories – 43 | Fat - 4g | Carbs - 9g | Protein - 5g | Sugar – 1g | Fiber – 1.5g | Potassium - 190mg | Sodium – 220mg | Cholesterol – 15mg

12.8 Chinese Spring Rolls

Preparation Time: 5 mins |

Cooking Time: 8 mins | Serving: 20

Ingredients:

- Minced beef or pork – 10 oz (284 g)
- Mixed vegetables – 7 oz (198 g)
- Onion - 1 (diced)
- Garlic - 3 cloves (minced)
- Dried rice noodles – 5 oz (142 g)
- Sesame oil – 1 tsp (5 ml)
- Vegetable oil – 1 tbsp (15 ml)
- Soy sauce – 1 tsp (5 ml)
- Egg roll wrappers – 1 pack

Method:

1. Cook the minced beef/pork, onion, garlic, and vegetables for 6 minutes in a pan
2. Add the noodles and soy sauce and combine
3. Add some of the mixture to each egg roll wrap and fold in the middle section and corners. Roll and brush with the egg to seal the edges
4. Coat lightly in vegetable oil and place in the air fryer
5. Cos for 8 minutes at 190°C (370°F)

Nutrition per serving:

Calories – 190 | Fat - 4g | Carbs - 9g | Protein - 5g | Sugar - 2g | Fiber - 1g | Potassium - 200mg | Sodium – 310mg | Cholesterol – 10mg

12.9 Jalapeño & Cream Cheese Pops

Preparation Time: 5 mins |

Cooking Time: 8 mins | Serving: 6

Ingredients:
- Jalapeños - 10
- Breadcrumbs – 5 oz (142 g)
- Parsley – 1.7 oz (48 g) (chopped)
- Cream cheese – 3.5 oz (99 g)

Method:
1. Combine half the breadcrumbs with the cream cheese
2. Stir in the chopped parsley
3. Stuff the jalapeños with the mixture and sprinkle the rest of the breadcrumbs over the top
4. Cook in the air fryer for 6-8 minutes at 180°C (350°F)

Nutrition per serving:

Calories – 190 | Fat - 4g | Carbs - 9g | Protein - 5g | Sugar – 2g | Fiber – 2g | Potassium - 180mg | Sodium – 250mg | Cholesterol – 20mg

12.10 Fragrant Onion Pakora

Preparation Time: 5 mins |

Cooking Time: 10 mins | Serving: 6

Ingredients:
- Onions – 2 (sliced)
- Gram flour – 7 oz (198 g)
- Crushed coriander seeds – 1 tbsp (15 g)
- Chili powder – 1 tsp (5 g)
- Salt – 1 tsp (5 g)
- Turmeric – 0.24 tsp (1.5 g)
- Baking soda – 0.25 tsp (1.5 g)

Method:
1. Combine all ingredients until smooth
2. Use your hands to make ball shapes
3. Line the inside of the fryer basket with cooking foil
4. Arrange the pakoras inside and cook for 5 minutes at 200°C (390°F)
5. Turn and cook for another 5 minutes

Nutrition per serving:

Calories – 185 | Fat - 15g | Carbs - 21g | Protein - 9g | Sugar - 1g | Fiber - 3g | Potassium - 190mg | Sodium – 410mg | Cholesterol – 0mg

12.11 Bacon & Balsamic Sprouts

Preparation Time: 5 mins |

Cooking Time: 10 mins | Serving: 2

Ingredients:
- Bacon – 2 tsp (10 g) (crumbled)
- Brussels sprouts – 140 oz (396 g) (halved)
- Avocado oil – 1 tbsp (15 ml)
- Balsamic vinegar – 1 tsp (5 ml)
- Salt and pepper – to taste

Method:
1. Mix the seasoning and oil together in a bowl
2. Add the sprouts and make sure they are covered completely in the mixture
3. Cook for 5 minutes at 180°C (350°F)
4. Shake well and continue to cook for a further 5 minutes
5. Serve with bacon and balsamic vinegar over the top

Nutrition per serving:
Calories – 100 | Fat - 9g | Carbs - 13g | Protein - 5g | Sugar – 2g | Fiber - 4g | Potassium - 200mg | Sodium – 340mg | Cholesterol – 12mg

12.12 Cheesy, Garlic Asparagus

Preparation Time: 5 mins |

Cooking Time: 10 mins | Serving: 4

Ingredients:
- Asparagus – 17 oz (481 g) (trimmed)
- Parmesan cheese – 1 tbsp (15 g) (shredded)
- Olive oil – 1 tsp (5 g)
- Garlic salt – 1 tsp (5 g)
- Salt and pepper – to taste

Method:
1. Place the asparagus into the air fryer and drizzle a little oil over the top
2. Add the garlic salt and shredded parmesan, with as much seasoning as you prefer
3. Cook at 200°C (390°F) for 10 minutes

Nutrition per serving:
Calories – 296 | Fat - 3g | Carbs - 12g | Protein - 11g | Sugar – 2g | Fiber - 3g | Potassium - 210mg | Sodium – 320mg | Cholesterol – 5mg

12.13 Spicy Corn on The Cob

Preparation Time: 5 mins |

Cooking Time: 8 mins | Serving: 4

Ingredients:
- Corn cobs – 2 (halved)
- Cheese – 2 tsp (10 g) (shredded)
- Mayonnaise – 2.6 oz (73 g)
- Chili powder – 0.25 tsp (1 g)
- Lime juice – 1 tsp (5 ml)

Method:
1. Combine the lime juice, chili powder, shredded cheese, and mayonnaise in a large bowl
2. Coat the corn in the mixture on all sides
3. Cook for 8 minutes at 200°C (390°F)

Nutrition per serving:

Calories – 196 | Fat - 15g | Carbs - 21g | Protein - 11g | Sugar – 2g | Fiber – 2.5g | Potassium - 250mg | Sodium – 150mg | Cholesterol – 12mg

12.14 Parsley Snack Potatoes

Preparation Time: 5 mins |

Cooking Time: 25 mins | Serving: 4

Ingredients:
- Olive oil – 1 tbsp (15 ml)
- Baby potatoes – 17 oz (481 g) (quartered)
- Parsley – 0.5 tsp (2.5 g) (dried)
- Garlic powder – 0.5 tsp (2.5 g)
- Salt – 1 tsp (5 g)

Method:
1. Mix together the olive oil and potatoes in a large mixing bowl
2. Add the parsley, salt, and garlic powder, and coat the potatoes completely
3. Cook for 25 minutes in the air fryer at 180°C (350°F)
4. , turning at the halfway point

Nutrition per serving:

Calories – 100 | Fat - 0.3g | Carbs - 20g | Protein - 2g | Sugar - 2g | Fiber - 2g | Potassium - 220mg | Sodium – 300mg | Cholesterol – 0mg

12.15 Eggplant Snacks

Preparation Time: 5 mins |

Cooking Time: 12 mins | Serving: 4

Ingredients:
- Eggplant – 1 (sliced)
- Eggs - 2
- Flour – 3.5 oz (99 g)
- Parmesan cheese – 7 oz (198 g) (shredded)
- Breadcrumbs – 3.5 oz (99 g)
- Black pepper – 0.5 tsp (2.5 g)
- Onion powder – 0.5 tsp (2.5 g)
- Salt – 1 tsp (5 g)
- Basil – 0.5 tsp (2.5 g) (dried)
- Italian seasoning – 1 tsp (5 g)

Method:
1. Place the cheese, seasoning, and breadcrumbs in a bowl and mix with a fork
2. Take another bowl and add the flour
3. Add the egg to another bowl and beat
4. Take the eggplant and dip into the flour, eggs, and then the breadcrumb mixture
5. Cook in the air fryer at 180°C (370°F) for 8 minutes
6. Turn and cook for another 4 minutes

Nutrition per serving:
Calories – 200 | Fat - 4.9g | Carbs - 33.2g | Protein - 9.4g | Sugar – 2g | Fiber – 4.2g | Potassium - 257mg | Sodium – 512mg | Cholesterol – 87mg

12.16 Snack Chickpeas

Preparation Time: 10 mins |

Cooking Time: 8 mins | Serving: 5

Ingredients:
- Drained chickpeas – 1 can
- White vinegar – 0.5 cups (118 ml)
- Olive oil – 1 tbsp (15 ml)
- Salt – to taste

Method:
1. Place the vinegar and chickpeas in a pan
2. Over a medium heat, combine and simmer for a few minutes
3. Allow to rest for 30 minutes, away from the heat
4. Place the chickpeas in the air fryer and cook at 180°C (370°F) for 4 minutes
5. Transfer to an ovenproof bowl
6. Add seasoning and the oil and combine
7. Place the bowl into the air fryer and cook for 4 minutes

Nutrition per serving:
Calories – 230 | Fat - 8g | Carbs - 32g | Protein - 6g | Sugar – 3g | Fiber – 8g | Potassium - 170mg | Sodium – 180mg | Cholesterol – 0mg

12.17 Zingy Shishito Peppers

Preparation Time: 5 mins |

Cooking Time: 25 mins | Serving: 2

Ingredients:
- Shishito peppers – 7 oz (198 g)
- Limes - 2
- Shredded cheese – 2.6 oz (73 g)
- Avocado oil – 0.5 tbsp (7.5 ml)
- Salt and pepper – to taste

Method:
1. Take a large bowl and add the oil, seasoning, and the peppers
2. Combine well
3. Place inside the fryer and cook for 10 minutes at 180°C (370°F)
4. Allow the cheese to melt on top of the peppers before serving

Nutrition per serving:

Calories – 256 | Fat - 11.4g | Carbs - 20.6g | Protein - 10.4g | Sugar – 3.6g | Fiber – 6.4g | Potassium - 578mg | Sodium – 460mg | Cholesterol – 24mg

12.18 Potatoes with Spinach

Preparation Time: 10 mins |

Cooking Time: 65 mins | Serving: 4

Ingredients:
- Olive oil – 2 tsp (10 ml)
- Spinach – 1.7 oz (48 g) (chopped)
- Potatoes - 2
- Yogurt – 0.5 cups (118 g)
- Whole milk – 0.5 cups (118 g)
- Salt and pepper – to taste

Method:
1. Take the potatoes and coat them slightly in oil
2. Place in the fryer and cook at 370°F (190°C) for 30 minutes
3. Turnover and cook for a further 30 minutes
4. Remove the middle of the potatoes using a spoon and mash with the yogurt and milk
5. Add the seasoning and spinach and mix until everything is incorporated
6. Place the mixture back inside the potato skins
7. Place back in the air fryer and cook at 320°F (160°C) for 5 minutes

Nutrition per serving:

Calories – 416 | Fat - 14.2g | Carbs - 59.2g | Protein - 15.2g | Sugar – 7.6g | Fiber – 8.4g | Potassium - 1250mg | Sodium – 360mg | Cholesterol – 30mg

12.19 Zucchini Snack Gratin

Preparation Time: 5 mins |

Cooking Time: 15 mins | Serving: 2

Ingredients:
- Olive oil – 1 tbsp (15 ml)
- Zucchini – 2 (slices)
- Breadcrumbs – 2 tbsp (30 g)
- Chopped parsley – 1 tbsp (15 g)
- Shredded parmesan – 4 tbsp (60 g)
- Salt and pepper – To taste (seasoning)

Method:
1. Take a large bowl and combine all ingredients except the sliced zucchini
2. Arrange the sliced zucchini inside the air fryer and add the combined mixture on the top
3. Cook for 15 minutes at 180°C (350°F)

Nutrition per serving:
Calories – 183 | Fat - 11.6g | Carbs - 13.8g | Protein - 7.2g | Sugar – 2.4g | Fiber – 2.5g | Potassium - 451mg | Sodium – 523mg | Cholesterol – 31mg

12.20 Air Fryer Dill Pickles

Preparation Time: 10 mins |

Cooking Time: 8 mins | Serving: 4

Ingredients:
- Dill pickles – 1 jar (slices)
- Whole milk – 2 tbsp (30 g)
- Egg - 1
- Mayonnaise – 0.5 cups (118 ml)
- Flour - 1.7 oz (48 g)
- Cornmeal – 1.7 oz (48 g)
- Sriracha sauce – 2 tsp (10 g)
- Paprika – 0.25 tsp (1 g)
- Salt – 0.5 tsp (2.5 g)
- Pepper – 0.5 tsp (2.5 g)
- Garlic powder – 0.25 tsp (1 g)

Method:
1. Combine the sriracha sauce and mayonnaise and place to one side
2. Take another bowl and combine the milk and egg
3. In another bowl, add the rest of the ingredients, except for the dill pickles, and combine
4. Take the pickles and first dip into the egg and then the flour
5. Place in the air fryer and cook for 4 minutes at 200°C (390°F)

Nutrition per serving:
Calories – 170 | Fat - 12.8g | Carbs - 11.6g | Protein - 2.7g | Sugar – 2.1g | Fiber – 0.7g | Potassium - 109mg | Sodium – 976mg | Cholesterol – 56mg

13 MEAL PLAN

Welcome to the Air Fryer Diet Cookbook, featuring a 10-Week Healthy Meal Plan curated by our Licensed Practicing Dietitian. Dive into daily spreads of 3 main meals and 2 snacks, each enriched with nutrients provided with per day distribution. But remember, everyone's body is its own marvel, with unique mechanisms and potential co-morbidities. While this book offers a nourishing road map, it's not a universal fix. Let this be your inspiration for a starting point, inspiring a healthier you, not the ultimate answer.

12.21 Week 1

Monday
Breakfast 2.1 French Toast (Cal 332, p.11)
Snack 6.1Crunchy Ranch Potatoes (Cal 390, p.45)
Lunch 4.1 Aubergine Parmesan (Cal 690, p.29)
Snack 10.1Classic Lamb Patties (Cal 478, p.68)
Dinner 3.1 Shrimp Pops (Cal 332, p.21)
Nutrition Per Day
Calories – 2222 | Fat - 48g | Carbs - 107g | Protein - 39g | Sugar – 18g | Fiber – 11g | Potassium - 1214mg | Sodium – 1760mg | Cholesterol – 487mg

Tuesday
Breakfast 2.2Air Fryer Eggs (Cal 300, p.11)
Snack 6.2 Cheesy Carrot Chips (Cal 300, p.45)
Lunch 4.2 Citrus Flower (Cal 550, p.29)
Snack 10.2 Lamb and Worcestershire Sauce Peppers (Cal 332, p.68)
Dinner 3.2Crab Stuffed Mushrooms (Cal 500, p.21)
Nutrition Per Day
Calories – 1982 | Fat - 47g | Carbs - 88g | Protein - 43g | Sugar – 7g | Fiber – 14.3g | Potassium - 1193mg | Sodium – 2200mg | Cholesterol – 605mg

Wednesday
Breakfast 2.3 Easy Pancakes (Cal 250, p.12)
Snack 6.3 Spicy Rice (Cal 400, p.46)
Lunch 4.3 Cheese Tika (Cal 690, p.30)
Snack 10.3 Lamb and Jalapeno Empanadas (Cal 300, p.69)
Dinner 3.3 Zingy Shrimp (Cal 400, p.22)
Nutrition Per Day
Calories – 2040 | Fat - 53g | Carbs - 100g | Protein - 39g | Sugar – 10g | Fiber – 11g | Potassium - 1015mg | Sodium – 1475mg | Cholesterol – 575mg

Thursday
Breakfast 2.4 Morning Wraps (Cal 450, p.12)
Snack 6.4 Garlic Asparagus (Cal 200, p.46)
Lunch 4.4 Air Fryer Ravioli (Cal 456, p.30)
Snack 10.4 Lamb Kebabs (Cal 290, p.69)
Dinner 3.4 Easy Bread Crumbed Fish (Cal 600, p.22)
Nutrition Per Day
Calories – 1996 | Fat - 47g | Carbs - 77g | Protein - 38g | Sugar – 11g | Fiber – 13.2g | Potassium - 1090mg | Sodium – 2260mg | Cholesterol – 369mg

Friday
Breakfast 2.5 Cheese & Ham in Puff Pastry (Cal 450, p.13)
Snack 6.5 Tasty Potato Wedges (Cal 210, p.47)
Lunch 4.5 Falafel Patties (Cal 445, p.31)
Snack 10.5 Lamb and Ginger Burgers (Cal 392, p.70)
Dinner 3.5 Asian Fish Patties (Cal 553, p.23)
Nutrition Per Day
Calories – 2050 | Fat - 47g | Carbs - 99g | Protein - 37g | Sugar – 6g | Fiber – 10.1g | Potassium - 1635mg | Sodium – 1550mg | Cholesterol – 475mg

Saturday
Breakfast 2.6"Spanish" Frittata (Cal 46, p.13)
Snack 6.6 Avocado Chips (Cal 380, p.47)
Lunch 4.6 Mushroom Pasta (Cal 450, p.31)
Snack 10.6 Cheesy Lamb Balls (Cal 200, p.70)
Dinner 3.6 Simple Fish Fingers (Cal 655, p.23)
Nutrition Per Day
Calories – 2698 | Fat - 52g |Carbs - 139g | Protein - 49g | Sugar – 9g | Fiber – 16.6g | Potassium - 1795mg | Sodium – 2245mg | Cholesterol – 616mg

Sunday
Breakfast 2.7 Ham & Egg Bites (Cal 450, p.14)
Snack 6.7 Fruity Tofu (Cal 190, p.48)
Lunch 4.7 Courgette Rolls (Cal 400, p.32)
Snack 10.7 Spicy Lamb Balls (Cal 290, p.72)
Dinner 3.7 Salmon Burgers (Cal 590, p.24)
Nutrition Per Day
Calories – 1920 | Fat - 37g | Carbs - 106g | Protein - 35g | Sugar – 11g | Fiber – 11.6g | Potassium - 1347mg | Sodium – 1600mg | Cholesterol – 638mg

12.22 Week 2

Monday
Breakfast 2.8 Vegetable Hash Browns (Cal 400, p.14)
Snack 6.8 Parsley Courgette (Cal 290, p.48)
Lunch 4.8 Cheese and Pasta Quiche (Cal 440, p.32)
Snack 10.8 Mushroom and Onion Patties (Cal 353, p.72)
Dinner 3.8 Spicy Shrimp Roll (Cal 450, p.24)
Nutrition Per Day
Calories – 1933 | Fat - 54g | Carbs - 96g | Protein - 30g | Sugar – 8g | Fiber – 15.2g | Potassium - 1115mg | Sodium – 2310mg | Cholesterol – 372mg

Tuesday
Breakfast 2.9 Air Fryer Omelet (Cal 280, p.15)
Snack 6.9 Stuffed Pumpkin (Cal 180, p.49)
Lunch 4.9 Lentil Balls (Cal 500, p.33)
Snack 10.9 Lasagna Taco Bake (Cal 390, p.72)
Dinner 3.9 Fish Taco Bowl (Cal 600, p.25)
Nutrition Per Day
Calories – 1950 | Fat - 74g | Carbs - 105g | Protein - 43g | Sugar – 10g | Fiber – 21.6g | Potassium - 1940mg | Sodium – 1820mg | Cholesterol – 650mg

Wednesday
Breakfast 2.10 Full & Healthy Peppers (Cal 450, p.15)
Snack 6.10 Marinated Cauliflower (Cal 190, p.49)
Lunch 4.10 Air Fryer Vegetable Bake (Cal 400, p.33)
Snack 10.10 Lamb and Parsley Roll (Cal 440, p.72)
Dinner 3.10 Air Fryer Scallops (Cal 500, p.25)
Nutrition Per Day
Calories – 1980 | Fat - 54g | Carbs - 103g | Protein - 41g | Sugar – 11g | Fiber – 12.3g | Potassium - 1320mg | Sodium – 1660mg | Cholesterol – 885mg

Thursday
Breakfast 2.11 Sausage Surprise (Cal 470, p.15)
Snack 9.1 Steak & Asparagus Cubes (Cal 486, p.63)
Lunch 4.11 Mediterranean Gnocchi (Cal 590, p.34)
Snack 12.11 Cheesy Garlic Bites (Cal 225, p.78)
Dinner 3.11 Air Fryer Mussels (Cal 332, p.26)
Nutrition Per Day
Calories – 2103 | Fat - 69g | Carbs - 138g | Protein - 35g | Sugar – 17.5g | Fiber – 10.3g | Potassium - 1025mg | Sodium – 2430mg | Cholesterol – 287.5mg

Friday

Breakfast 2.12 Cheesy Toast (Cal 450, p.16)
Snack 9.2 Mexican Steak and Chip (Cal 436, p.63)
Lunch 4.12 Healthy Vegetarian Pizza (Cal 390, p.34)
Snack 12.2 Chicken and Bacon BBQ Bites (Cal 250, p.78)
Dinner 3.2 Boozy Fish Tacos (Cal 332, p.26)
Nutrition Per Day
Calories – 1858 | Fat - 39g | Carbs - 86g | Protein - 31g | Sugar – 17g | Fiber – 10.1g | Potassium - 1090mg | Sodium – 2450mg | Cholesterol – 380mg

Saturday

Breakfast 2.13 **Breakfast** Sandwich (Cal 300, p.17)
Snack 9.3 Beef Wellington (Cal 256, p.64)
Lunch 4.13 Air Fryer Tofu (Cal 200, p.35)
Snack 12.3 Onion Bhajis (Cal 290, p.79)
Dinner 3.13 Herby Tilapia (Cal 650, p.27)
Nutrition Per Day
Calories – 1696 | Fat - 48g | Carbs - 68g | Protein - 37g | Sugar – 9g | Fiber – 8.7g | Potassium - 1070mg | Sodium – 1760mg | Cholesterol – 330mg

12.23 Week 3

Monday

Breakfast 2.15 Spinach & Eggs (Cal 350, p.18)
Snack 9.5 Beef Fried Rice (Cal 325, p.65)
Lunch 4.15 Potato Gratin (Cal 400, p.36)
Snack 12.5 Stringy Mozzarella Sticks (Cal 686, p.80)
Dinner 3.15 Coconut Shrimp (Cal 630, p.28)
Nutrition Per Day
Calories – 2391 | Fat - 112g | Carbs - 104g | Protein - 43g | Sugar – 14g | Fiber – 14.5g | Potassium - 3860mg | Sodium – 1870mg | Cholesterol – 520mg

Sunday

Breakfast 2.14 Quick Morning Doughnuts (Cal 332, p.17)
Snack 9.4 Coco Nut Asian Beef (Cal 356, p.64)
Lunch 4.14 Creamy Pasta Bake (Cal 450, p.35)
Snack 12.4 Spicy Pork Bites (Cal 292, p.79)
Dinner 3.14 Tartar Battered Fish Sticks (Cal 690, p.27)
Nutrition Per Day
Calories – 2120 | Fat - 77g | Carbs - 94g | Protein - 45g | Sugar – 24g | Fiber – 7.7g | Potassium - 1270mg | Sodium – 1940mg | Cholesterol – 295mg

Tuesday

Breakfast 2.16 Breakfast Pockets (Cal 500, p.18)
Snack 9.6 Feta Hamburgers (Cal 334, p.65)
Lunch 5.1 Artichoke and Pumpkin Seed Pasta (Cal 400, p.37)
Snack 12.6 Picnic Scotch Eggs (Cal 407, p.80)
Dinner 7.1 Turkey in Mushroom Sauce (Cal 426, p.50)
Nutrition Per Day
Calories – 2067 | Fat - 60g | Carbs - 65g | Protein - 34g | Sugar – 6g | Fiber – 8.5g | Potassium - 1520mg | Sodium – 2250mg | Cholesterol – 568mg

Wednesday

Breakfast 2.17 Easy Boiled Eggs (Cal 400, p.19)
Snack 9.7 Stuffed Peppers with Beef (Cal 332, p.66)
Lunch 5.2 Jackfruit Taquitos (Cal 380, p.37)
Snack 12.7 Cheesy Carrot Mushrooms (Cal 43, p.81)
Dinner 7.2 zingy Lemon Chicken Wings (Cal 356, p.50)

Nutrition Per Day
Calories – 1511 | Fat - 23g | Carbs - 74g | Protein - 32g | Sugar – 10g | Fiber – 13.7g | Potassium - 955mg | Sodium – 1230mg | Cholesterol – 909mg

Thursday

Breakfast 2.18 Paprika Hash (Cal 650, p.19)
Snack 9.8 Paprika Steak and Mushroom (Cal 190, p.66)
Lunch 5.3 Air Fryer Perogies (Cal 690, p.38)
Snack 12.8 Chinese Spring Rolls (Cal 190, p.81)
Dinner 7.3 Air Fryer Potatoes with Chicken (Cal 390, p.51)

Nutrition Per Day
Calories – 2110 | Fat - 45g | Carbs - 98g | Protein - 38g | Sugar – 12g | Fiber – 13.1g | Potassium - 1390mg | Sodium – 2150mg | Cholesterol – 190mg

Friday

Breakfast 2.19 Egg "Sandwiches" (Cal 332, p.20)
Snack 9.9 Beef Enchiladas (Cal 546, p.67)
Lunch 5.4 Radish Browns (Cal 360, p.38)
Snack 12.9 Jalapeno and Cream Cheese Pops (Cal 190, p.82)
Dinner 7.4 Spicy Tandoori Chicken (Cal 500, p.51)

Nutrition Per Day
Calories – 1928 | Fat - 42g | Carbs - 93g | Protein - 34g | Sugar – 17g | Fiber – 15.1g | Potassium - 1210mg | Sodium – 1900mg | Cholesterol – 314mg

Saturday

Breakfast 2.20 Creamy Breakfast Treats (Cal 450, p.20)
Snack 9.10 Spicy Steak Wraps (Cal 220, p.67)
Lunch 5.5 Lentil and Cabbage Patties (Cal 400, p. 39)
Snack 12.10 Fragrant Onion Pakora (Cal 185, p.82)
Dinner 7.5 Turkey and Mushroom Burgers (Cal 360, p.52)

Nutrition Per Day
Calories – 1615 | Fat - 41g | Carbs - 84g | Protein - 36g | Sugar – 8g | Fiber – 15.4g | Potassium - 1350mg | Sodium – 1830mg | Cholesterol – 242mg

Sunday

Breakfast 11.1 Vanilla Biscuit (Cal 226, p.73)
Snack 6.1 Crunchy Ranch Potatoes (Cal 390, p.45)
Lunch 5.6 Courgette and Coriander Burger (Cal 440, p.39)
Snack 12.11 Bacon and Balsamic Sprout (Cal 100, p.83)
Dinner 7.6 Smoked Chicken (Cal 432, p.52)

Nutrition Per Day
Calories – 1588 | Fat - 32g | Carbs - 63g | Protein - 24g | Sugar – 8g | Fiber – 13.8g | Potassium - 1100mg | Sodium – 1470mg | Cholesterol – 127mg

12.24 Week 4

Monday

Breakfast 11.2 Orange Cocoa Dip (Cal 400, p.73)
Snack 6.2 Cheesy Carrot Chips (Cal 300, p.45)
Lunch 5.7 Vegan Cheese and Bread Sticks (Cal 490, p.40)
Snack 12.12 Cheesy, Garlic Asparagus (Cal 296, p.83)
Dinner 7.7 Chicken Thighs in Bacon (Cal 390, p.53)
Nutrition Per Day
Calories – 1876 | Fat - 58g | Carbs - 76g | Protein - 42g | Sugar – 8g | Fiber – 9.1g | Potassium - 1190mg | Sodium – 1465mg | Cholesterol – 153mg

Tuesday

Breakfast 11.3 Delicious Profiteroles (Cal 390, p.74)
Snack 6.3 Spicy Rice (Cal 400, p.46)
Lunch 5.8 Canarian Potatoes (Cal 390, p.40)
Snack 12.13 Spicy Corn on The Cob (Cal 196, p.84)
Dinner 7.8 Chicken with A Bang (Cal 450, p.53)
Nutrition Per Day
Calories – 1826 | Fat - 76g | Carbs - 93g | Protein - 38g | Sugar – 9g | Fiber – 9.4g | Potassium - 1180mg | Sodium – 1550mg | Cholesterol – 197mg

Wednesday

Breakfast 11.4 Cherry Parcel (Cal 290, p.74)
Snack 6.4 Garlic Asparagus (Cal 200, p.46)
Lunch 5.9 Cheesy Bagel Pizza (Cal 690, p.41)
Snack 12.14 Parsley **Snack** Potatoes (Cal 100, p.84)
Dinner 7.9 Chicken Fried Rice (Cal 390, p.54)
Nutrition Per Day
Calories – 1670 | Fat - 39.3g | Carbs - 133g | Protein - 37g | Sugar – 9g | Fiber – 11.4g | Potassium - 1080mg | Sodium – 2160mg | Cholesterol – 49mg

Thursday

Breakfast 11.5 Classic Creamy Cheesecake (Cal 831, p.75)
Snack 6.5 Tasty Potatoes Wedges (Cal 210, p.47)
Lunch 5.10 Pumpkin and Lemon Pasta (Cal 500, p.41)
Snack 12.15 Eggplant **Snack**s (Cal 200, p. 85)
Dinner 7.10 Sticky Chicken Thighs (Cal 550, p.54)
Nutrition Per Day
Calories – 2291 | Fat - 72.9g | Carbs - 105.2g | Protein - 37.8g | Sugar – 8g | Fiber – 11.9g | Potassium - 1567mg | Sodium – 1347mg | Cholesterol – 347mg

Friday

Breakfast 11.6 Classic Apple Pie (Cal 486, p.75)
Snack 6.6 Avocado Chips (Cal 380, p.47)
Lunch 5.12 Crostini with Artichoke (Cal 440, p.42)
Snack 12.16 **Snack** Chickpeas (Cal 230, p.85)
Dinner 7.11 Cayenne Wings (Cal 730, p.55)
Nutrition Per Day
Calories – 2266 | Fat - 95g | Carbs - 71g | Protein - 80g | Sugar – 14g | Fiber – 19g | Potassium - 1440mg | Sodium – 1590mg | Cholesterol – 359mg

Saturday

Breakfast 11.7 Chocolate Soufflé (Cal 486, p.76)
Snack 6.7 Fruity Tofu (Cal 190, p.48)
Lunch 5.12 Cheesy Baked Potatoes (Cal 330, p.42)
Snack 12.17 Zingy Shishito Pepper (Cal 256, p.86)
Dinner 7.12 Easy Chicken Nuggets (Cal 213, p.55)
Nutrition Per Day
Calories – 1838 | Fat - 76.2g | Carbs - 144.2g | Protein - 58.2g | Sugar – 16.6g | Fiber – 19g | Potassium - 2705mg | Sodium – 1590mg | Cholesterol – 210mg

Sunday
Breakfast 11.8 Classic Chocolate Cake (Cal 573, p.76)
Snack 6.8 Parsley Courgette (Cal 290, p.48)
Lunch 5.13 BBQ Soy Curl (Cal 190, p.43)
Snack 12.18 Potatoes with Spinach (Cal 416, p.46)
Dinner 7.13 Chicken and Jalapeno Chimichangas (Cal 406, p.56)
Nutrition Per Day
Calories – 1875 | Fat - 79.2g | Carbs - 133.2g | Protein - 55.2g | Sugar – 16.6g | Fiber – 17g | Potassium - 2185mg | Sodium – 1640mg | Cholesterol – 152mg

12.25 Week 5

Monday
Breakfast 11.9 Honey & Apple Pasties (Cal 190, p.77)
Snack 6.9 Stuffed Pumpkin (Cal 180, p.49)
Lunch 5.14 Onion Arancini (Cal 690, p.43)
Snack 12.19 Zucchini **Snack** Gratin (Cal 183, p.87)
Dinner 7.14 Paprika and Garlic Chicken (Cal 305, p.56)
Nutrition Per Day
Calories – 1548 | Fat - 48.6g | Carbs - 89.8g | Protein - 51.2g | Sugar – 12.4g | Fiber – 11g | Potassium - 1946mg | Sodium – 1663mg | Cholesterol – 206mg

Tuesday
Breakfast 11.10 Banana & Walnut Bread (Cal 326, p.77)
Snack 6.10 Marinated Cauliflower (Cal 190, p.49)
Lunch 5.15 Sweet Potato Wraps (Cal 400, p.44)
Snack 12.20 Air Fryer Dill Pickles (Cal 170, p.87)
Dinner 7.15 Turkey Bites (Cal 213, p.57)
Nutrition Per Day:
Calories – 1559 | Fat - 61.8g | Carbs - 96.6g | Protein - 50.7g | Sugar – 31.1g | Fiber – 5.5g | Potassium - 945mg | Sodium – 2196mg | Cholesterol – 262mg

Wednesday
Breakfast 11.1 Vanilla Biscuits (Cal 226, p.73)
Snack 9.1 Steak and Asparagus Cubes (Cal 486, p.63)
Lunch 4.1 Aubergine Parmesan (Cal 490, p.29)
Snack 12.1 Cheesy Garlic Bread (Cal 225, p.78)
Dinner 8.1 Pork Tenderloin in Dijon Mustard (Cal 450, p.58)
Nutrition Per Day
Calories – 2077 | Fat - 74g | Carbs - 104g | Protein - 68g | Sugar – 17g | Fiber – 12.1g | Potassium - 1260mg | Sodium – 2200mg | Cholesterol – 357mg

Thursday
Breakfast 11.2 Orange Cocoa Dip (Cal 400, p.7)
Snack 9.2 Mexican Steak and Chip (Cal 436, p.63)
Lunch 4.2 Citrus Cauliflower (Cal 550, p.29)
Snack 12.2 Chicken and Bacon BBQ Bites (Cal 250, p.78)
Dinner 8.2 Breaded Pork Chops (Cal 300, p.58)
Nutrition Per Day:
Calories – 1936 | Fat - 75g | Carbs - 83g | Protein - 53g | Sugar – 7g | Fiber – 11.8g | Potassium - 1290mg | Sodium – 2215mg | Cholesterol – 258mg

Friday
Breakfast 11.3 Delicious Profiteroles (Cal 390, p.74)
Snack 9.3 Coconut Wellington (Cal 256, p.64)
Lunch 4.3 Cheese Tikka (Cal 690, p.30)
Snack 12.3 Onion Bhajis (Cal 290, p.79)
Dinner 8.3 Pork and Marinara Sub (Cal 554, p.59)
Nutrition Per Day:
Calories – 2016 | Fat - 71g | Carbs - 83g | Protein - 58g | Sugar – 9g | Fiber – 12.7g | Potassium - 1340mg | Sodium – 1640mg | Cholesterol – 300mg

Saturday
Breakfast 11.4 Cherry Parcels (Cal 290, p.74)
Snack 9.4 Coconut Asian Beef (Cal 356, p.65)
Lunch 4.4 Air Fryer Ravioli (Cal 456, p.30)
Snack 12.4 Spicy Pork Bites (Cal 292, p.79)
Dinner 8.4 BBQ Ribs (Cal 554, p.59)
Nutrition Per Day:
Calories – 1948 | Fat - 73g | Carbs - 67g | Protein - 93g | Sugar – 33g | Fiber – 6.8g | Potassium - 1550mg | Sodium – 2370mg | Cholesterol – 250mg

Sunday
Breakfast 11.5 Classic Creamy Cheesecake (Cal 831, p.75)
Snack 9.5 Beef Fried Rice (Cal 325, p.65)
Lunch 4.5 Falafel Patties (Cal 445, p.31)
Snack 12.5 Stringy Mozzarella Bites (Cal 686, p.80)
Dinner 8.5 Pork Schnitzel (Cal 426, p.60)
Nutrition Per Day
Calories – 2713 | Fat - 132g | Carbs - 99g | Protein - 75g | Sugar – 7g | Fiber – 11.4g | Potassium - 3610mg | Sodium – 1700mg | Cholesterol – 390mg

12.26 Week 6

Monday
Breakfast 11.6 Classic Apple Pie (Cal 486, p.75)
Snack 9.6 Feta Hamburgers (Cal 334, p.65)
Lunch 4.6 Mushroom Pasta (Cal 450, p.31)
Snack 12.6 Picnic Scotch Eggs (Cal 407, p.80)
Dinner 8.6 Fruity Balsamic Pork Chops (Cal 579, p.60)
Nutrition Per Day:
Calories – 2256 | Fat - 100g | Carbs - 103g | Protein - 78g | Sugar – 23g | Fiber – 8.2g | Potassium - 1300mg | Sodium – 1900mg | Cholesterol – 492mg

Tuesday
Breakfast 11.7 Chocolate Soufflé (Cal 486, p.76)
Snack 9.7 Stuffed Peppers with Beef (Cal 332, p.66)
Lunch 4.7 Courgette Roll (Cal 400, p.32)
Snack 12.7 Cheesy Carrot Mushrooms (Cal 43, p.81)
Dinner 8.7 Chinese Spiced Pork (Cal 510, p.61)
Nutrition Per Day:
Calories – 1771 | Fat - 78g | Carbs - 88g | Protein - 67g | Sugar – 9g | Fiber – 12.9g | Potassium - 1260mg | Sodium – 1280mg | Cholesterol – 448mg

Wednesday

Breakfast 11.8 Classic Chocolate Cake (Cal 573, p.76)
Snack 9.8 Paprika Steak and Mushroom (Cal 190, p.66)
Lunch 4.8 Cheese and Pasta Quiche (Cal 440, p.32)
Snack 12.8 Chinese Spring Rolls (Cal 190, p.81)
Dinner 8.8 Pineapple Pork (Cal 256, p.61)
Nutrition Per Day:
Calories – 1649 | Fat - 60g | Carbs - 98g | Protein - 26g | Sugar – 9g | Fiber – 9g | Potassium - 1040mg | Sodium – 1630mg | Cholesterol – 285mg

Thursday

Breakfast 11.9 Honey & Apple Pasties (Cal 190, p.77)
Snack 9.9 Beef Enchiladas (Cal 546, p.67)
Lunch 4.9 Lentil Balls (Cal 500, p.33)
Snack 12.9 Jalapeno and Cream Cheese Pops (Cal 190, p.82)
Dinner 8.9 Seasoned Belly Pork (Cal 332, p.62)
Nutrition Per Day:
Calories – 1758 | Fat - 71g | Carbs - 72g | Protein - 38g | Sugar – 9g | Fiber – 16.6g | Potassium - 1490mg | Sodium – 1380mg | Cholesterol – 140mg

Friday

Breakfast 11.10 Banana & Walnut Bread (Cal 326, p.77)
Snack 9.1 Steak and Asparagus Cubes (Cal 486, p.63)
Lunch 4.10 Air Fryer Vegetable Bake (Cal 400, p.33)
Snack 12.10 Fragrant Onion Pakora (Cal 185, p.82)
Dinner 8.10 Pork and Ginger Meatballs (Cal 486, p.62)
Nutrition Per Day:
Calories – 1883 | Fat - 90g | Carbs - 141g | Protein - 48g | Sugar – 29g | Fiber – 16g | Potassium - 1216mg | Sodium – 1660mg | Cholesterol – 221mg

Saturday

Breakfast 2.1 French Toast (Cal 332, p.11)
Snack 9.2 Mexican Steak and Chips (Cal 436, p.63)
Lunch 4.11 Mediterranean Gnocchi (Cal 590, p.34)
Snack 12.11 Bacon and Balsamic Sprouts (Cal 100, p.83)
Dinner 7.1 Turkey in Mushroom Sauce (Cal 426, p.50)
Nutrition Per Day:
Calories – 1884 | Fat - 76g | Carbs - 112g | Protein - 31g | Sugar – 8g | Fiber – 12.8g | Potassium - 1134mg | Sodium – 1780mg | Cholesterol – 350mg

Sunday

Breakfast 2.2 Air Fryer Eggs (Cal 300, p.11)
Lunch 4.12 Healthy Vegetarian Pizza (Cal 390, p.34)
Snack 12.12 Cheesy, Garlic Asparagus (Cal 296, p.83)
Dinner 7.2 Zingy Lemon Chicken Wings (Cal 356, p.50)
Nutrition Per Day:
Calories – 1342 | Fat - 17g | Carbs - 68g | Protein - 29g | Sugar – 7g | Fiber – 8.2g | Potassium - 523mg | Sodium – 1260mg | Cholesterol – 545mg

12.27 Week 7

Monday

Breakfast 2.3 Easy Pancakes (Cal 250, p.12)
Snack 9.4 Coconut Asian Beef (Cal 356, p.64)
Lunch 4.13 Air Fryer Tofu (Cal 200, p.35)
Snack 12.13 Spicy Corn on The Cob (Cal 196, p.84)
Dinner 7.3 Air Fryer Potatoes with Chicken (Cal 390, p.51)
Nutrition Per Day:
Calories – 1392 | Fat - 69g | Carbs - 80g | Protein - 38g | Sugar – 18g | Fiber – 11.6g | Potassium - 1165mg | Sodium – 1640mg | Cholesterol – 387mg

Tuesday

Breakfast 2.4 Morning Wraps (Cal 450, p.12)
Snack 9.5 Beef Fried Rice (Cal 325, p.65)
Lunch 4.14 Creamy Pasta Bake (Cal 450, p.35)
Snack 12.14 Parsley **Snack** Potatoes (Cal 100, p.84)
Dinner 7.4 Spicy Tandoori Chicken (Cal 500, p.51)
Nutrition Per Day:
Calories – 1825 | Fat - 71.3g | Carbs - 89g | Protein - 35g | Sugar – 9g | Fiber – 14.1g | Potassium - 1020mg | Sodium – 1580mg | Cholesterol – 410mg

Wednesday

Breakfast 2.5 Cheese & Ham in Puff Pastry (Cal 450, p.13)
Snack 9.6 Feta Hamburgers (Cal 334, p.65)
Lunch 4.15 Potato Gratin (Cal 400, p.36)
Snack 12.15 Eggplant **Snack**s (Cal 200, p.85)
Dinner 7.5 Turkey and Mushroom Burgers (Cal 360, p.52)
Nutrition Per Day:
Calories – 1744 | Fat - 61.9g | Carbs - 102.2g | Protein - 38.4g | Sugar – 8g | Fiber – 9.6g | Potassium - 1112mg | Sodium – 1982mg | Cholesterol – 612mg

Thursday

Breakfast 11.2 Orange Cocoa Dip (Cal 400, p.7)
Snack 9.2 Mexican Steak and Chip (Cal 436, p.63)
Lunch 4.2 Citrus Cauliflower (Cal 550, p.29)
Snack 12.2 Chicken and Bacon BBQ Bites (Cal 250, p.78)
Dinner 8.2 Breaded Pork Chops (Cal 300, p.58)
Nutrition Per Day:
Calories – 1936 | Fat - 75g | Carbs - 83g | Protein - 53g | Sugar – 7g | Fiber – 11.8g | Potassium - 1290mg | Sodium – 2215mg | Cholesterol – 258mg

Friday

Breakfast 2.7 Ham & Egg Bites (Cal 450, p.14)
Snack 9.8 Paprika Steak and Mushroom (Cal 190, p.66)
Lunch 5.2 Jackfruit Taquitos (Cal 380, p.37)
Snack 10.2 Lamb and Worcestershire Sauce Peppers (Cal 332, p.68)
Dinner 7.7 Turkey and Mushroom Burgers (Cal 390, p.53)
Nutrition Per Day:
Calories – 1742 | Fat - 35g | Carbs - 71g | Protein - 39g | Sugar – 10g | Fiber – 15.1g | Potassium - 1227mg | Sodium – 1910mg | Cholesterol – 415mg

Saturday

Breakfast 2.8 Vegetable Hash Browns (Cal 400, p.14)
Snack 9.10 Spicy Steak Wraps (Cal 220, p.67)
Lunch 5.3 Air Fryer Pierogies (Cal 690, p.38)
Snack 10.3 Lamb and Jalapeno Empanadas (Cal 300, p.69)
Dinner 7.8 Chicken with A Bang (Cal 450, p.53)
Nutrition Per Day:
Calories – 2060 | Fat - 61g | Carbs - 99g | Protein - 44g | Sugar – 10g | Fiber – 17.5g | Potassium - 1245mg | Sodium – 2200mg | Cholesterol – 245mg

Sunday
Breakfast 2.9 Air Fryer Omelet (Cal 280, p.15)
Snack 6.1Crunchy Ranch Potatoes (Cal 390, p.45)
Lunch 5.4Radish Browns (Cal 360, p.38)
Snack 10.4 Lamb Kebabs (Cal 250, p.69)
Dinner 7.9 Chicken Fried Rice (Cal 390, p.54)
Nutrition Per Day:
Calories – 1710 | Fat - 41g | Carbs - 74g | Protein - 37g | Sugar – 8g | Fiber – 8.5g | Potassium - 1130mg | Sodium – 2370mg | Cholesterol – 450mg

12.28 Week 8

Monday
Breakfast 2.10Full & Healthy Peppers (Cal 450, p.15)
Snack 6.2Cheesy Carrot Chips (Cal 300, p.45)
Lunch 5.5Lentil and Cabbage Patties (Cal 400, p.39)
Snack 10.5 Lamb and Ginger Burgers (Cal 392, p.70)
Dinner 7.10Sticky Chicken Thighs (Cal 550, p.54)
Nutrition Per Day:
Calories – 2092 | Fat - 47g | Carbs - 80g | Protein - 38g | Sugar – 8g | Fiber – 15.8g | Potassium - 1140mg | Sodium – 1740mg | Cholesterol – 930mg

Tuesday
Breakfast 2.11 Sausage Surprise (Cal 470, p.16)
Snack 6.3Spicy Rice (Cal 400, p.46)
Lunch 5.6 Courgette and Coriander Burgers (Cal 440, p.39)
Snack 10.6 Cheesy Lamb Balls (Cal 200, p.70)
Dinner 7.11 Cayenne Wings (Cal 730, p.55)
Nutrition Per Day:
Calories – 2240 | Fat - 79g | Carbs - 84g | Protein - 82g | Sugar – 12.5g | Fiber – 11.8g | Potassium - 1135mg | Sodium – 2920mg | Cholesterol – 350mg

Wednesday
Breakfast 2.12Cheesy Toast (Cal 450, p.16)
Snack 6.4Garlic Asparagus (Cal 200, p.46)
Lunch 5.7Vegan Cheese with Bread Sticks (Cal 490, p.40)
Snack 10.7Spicy Lamb Meatballs (Cal 290, p.71)
Dinner 7.12 Easy Chicken Nuggets (Cal 213, p.55)
Nutrition Per Day:
Calories – 1643 | Fat - 58g | Carbs - 68g | Protein - 54g | Sugar – 11g | Fiber – 9.8g | Potassium - 810mg | Sodium – 1940mg | Cholesterol – 364mg

Thursday
Breakfast 2.13 **Breakfast** Sandwich (Cal 332, p.17)
Snack 6.5 Tasty Potatoes Wedges (Cal 210, p.47)
Lunch 5.8 Canarian Potatoes (Cal 390, p.40)
Snack 10.8 Mushroom and Onion Pasties (Cal 353, p.71)
Dinner 7.13 Chicken and Jalapeno Chimichangas (Cal 406, p.56)
Nutrition Per Day:
Calories – 1659 | Fat - 70g | Carbs - 103g | Protein - 53g | Sugar – 12g | Fiber – 13.2g | Potassium - 1105mg | Sodium – 1870mg | Cholesterol – 415mg

Friday
Breakfast 2.14 Quick Morning Doughnuts (Cal 332, p.17)
Snack 6.6 Avocado Chips (Cal 380, p.47)
Lunch 5.9 Cheesy Bagel Pizza (Cal 690, p.41)
Snack 10.9 Lasagna Taco Balls (Cal 390, p.72)
Dinner 7.14 Paprika and Garlic Chicken (Cal 305, p.56)
Nutrition Per Day:
Calories – 2097 | Fat - 54g | Carbs - 110g | Protein - 56g | Sugar – 16g | Fiber – 14.2g | Potassium - 1155mg | Sodium – 1950mg | Cholesterol – 299mg

Saturday
Breakfast 2.15 Spinach & Eggs (Cal 350, p.18)
Snack 6.7 Fruity Tofu (Cal 190, p.48)
Lunch 5.10 Pumpkin and Lemon Pizza (Cal 500, p.41)
Snack 10.10 Lamb and Parsley Rol (Cal 440, p.72)
Dinner 7.15 Turkey Bites (Cal 213, p.56)
Nutrition Per Day:
Calories – 1693 | Fat - 47g | Carbs - 72g | Protein - 52g | Sugar – 16g | Fiber – 10g | Potassium - 2290mg | Sodium – 1695mg | Cholesterol – 385mg

Sunday
Breakfast 2.16 Breakfast Pockets (Cal 500, p.18)
Snack 6.8 Parsley Courgette (Cal 290, p. 48)
Lunch 5.1 Crostini with Artichoke (Cal 440, p.42)
Snack 12.1 Cheesy Garlic Bread (Cal 225, p.78)
Dinner 3.1 Shrimp Pops (Cal 332, p.21)
Nutrition Per Day:
Calories – 1787 | Fat - 39g | Carbs - 64g | Protein - 28g | Sugar – 16g | Fiber – 6.6g | Potassium - 1000mg | Sodium – 2200mg | Cholesterol – 526.5mg

12.29 Week 9

Monday
Breakfast 2.17 Easy Boiled Eggs (Cal 400, p.19)
Snack 6.9 Stuffed Pumpkin (Cal 180, p.49)
Lunch 5.12 Cheesy Baked Potato (Cal 330, p.42)
Snack 12.2 Chicken and Bacon BBQ Bite (Cal 250, p.78)
Dinner 3.2 Crab Stuffed Mushrooms (Cal 500, p.21)
Nutrition Per Day:
Calories – 1660 | Fat - 38g | Carbs - 92g | Protein - 32g | Sugar – 10g | Fiber – 11.6g | Potassium - 2105mg | Sodium – 1630mg | Cholesterol – 994mg

Tuesday
Breakfast 2.18 Paprika Hash (Cal 650, p.19)
Snack 6.10 Marinated Cauliflower (Cal 190, p.49)
Lunch 5.13 BBQ Soy Curls (Cal 190, p.43)
Snack 12.3 Onion Bhajis (Cal 290, p.79)
Dinner 3.3 Zingy Shrimp (Cal 400, p.22)
Nutrition Per Day:
Calories – 1720 | Fat - 40g | Carbs - 79g | Protein - 35g | Sugar – 12g | Fiber – 11.6g | Potassium - 1690mg | Sodium – 1885mg | Cholesterol – 205mg

Wednesday

Breakfast 2.19 Egg "Sandwiches" (Cal 332, p.20)
Snack 9.1 Steak and Asparagus Cubes (Cal 486, p.63)
Lunch 5.14 Onion Arancini (Cal 690, p.43)
Snack 12.4 Spicy Pork Bites (Cal 292, p.79)
Dinner 3.4 Easy Bread Crumbed Fish (Cal 600, p.22)
Nutrition Per Day:
Calories – 2400 | Fat - 67g | Carbs - 111g | Protein - 42g | Sugar – 19g | Fiber – 10.2g | Potassium - 1430mg | Sodium – 2410mg | Cholesterol – 394mg

Thursday

Breakfast 2.20 Creamy **Breakfast** Treats (Cal 450, p.20)
Snack 9.3 Beef Wellington (Cal 256, p.64)
Lunch 5.15 Sweet Potato Wedges (Cal 400, p.44)
Snack 12.5 Stringy Mozzarella Sticks (Cal 686, p.80)
Dinner 3.5 Asian Fish Patties (Cal 553, p.23)
Nutrition Per Day:
Calories – 2345 | Fat - 49g | Carbs - 89g | Protein - 35g | Sugar – 9g | Fiber – 10.4g | Potassium - 3500mg | Sodium – 1880mg | Cholesterol – 312mg

Friday

Breakfast 2.1 French Toast (Cal 332, p.11)
Snack 9.4 Coconut Asian Beef (Cal 356, p.64)
Lunch 4.1 Aubergine Parmesan (Cal 690, p.29)
Snack 12.6 Picnic Scotch Eggs (Cal 407, p.80)
Dinner 3.6 Simple Fish Fingers (Cal 655, p.23)
Nutrition Per Day:
Calories – 2440 | Fat - 77g | Carbs - 117g | Protein - 44g | Sugar – 19g | Fiber – 13g | Potassium - 1304mg | Sodium – 2205mg | Cholesterol – 545mg

Saturday

Breakfast 2.2 Air Fryer Eggs (Cal 300, p.11)
Snack 9.5 Beef Fried Rice (Cal 325, p.65)
Lunch 4.2 Citrus Cauliflower (Cal 550, p.29)
Snack 12.7 Cheesy, Garlic Asparagus (Cal 43, p.81)
Dinner 3.7 Salmon Burgers (Cal 590, p.24)
Nutrition Per Day:
Calories – 1808 | Fat - 83g | Carbs - 99g | Protein - 36g | Sugar – 6g | Fiber – 12g | Potassium - 1143mg | Sodium – 1810mg | Cholesterol – 575mg

Sunday

Breakfast 2.2 Air Fryer Eggs (Cal 300, p.11)
Lunch 4.12 Healthy Vegetarian Pizza (Cal 390, p.34)
Snack 12.12 Cheesy, Garlic Asparagus (Cal 296, p.83)
Dinner 7.2 Zingy Lemon Chicken Wings (Cal 356, p.50)
Nutrition Per Day:
Calories – 1342 | Fat - 17g | Carbs - 68g | Protein - 29g | Sugar – 7g | Fiber – 8.2g | Potassium - 523mg | Sodium – 1260mg | Cholesterol – 545mg

12.30 Week 10

Monday
Breakfast 2.3 Easy Pancakes (Cal 250, p.12)
Snack 9.6 Feta Hamburgers (Cal 334, p.65)
Lunch 4.3 Cheese Tikka (Cal 690, p.30)
Snack 12.8 Chinese Spring Rolls (Cal 190, p.81)
Dinner 3.8 Spicy Shrimp Roll (Cal 450, p.24)
Nutrition Per Day:
Calories – 1914 | Fat - 56g | Carbs - 91g | Protein - 37g | Sugar – 9g | Fiber – 12.5g | Potassium - 1195mg | Sodium – 2140mg | Cholesterol – 490mg

Tuesday
Breakfast 2.4 Morning Wraps (Cal 450, p.12)
Snack 9.7 Stuffed Pepper with Beef (Cal 332, p.66)
Lunch 4.4 Air Fryer Ravioli (Cal 456, p.30)
Snack 12.9 Jalapeno and Cream Cheese Pops (Cal 190, p.82)
Dinner 3.9 Fish Taco Bowls (Cal 600, p.25)
Nutrition Per Day:
Calories – 2028 | Fat - 45g | Carbs - 78g | Protein - 34g | Sugar – 12g | Fiber – 19.8g | Potassium - 1160mg | Sodium – 1840mg | Cholesterol – 380Mg

Wednesday
Breakfast 2.5 Cheese & Ham in Puff Pastry (Cal 450, p.13)
Snack 9.8 Paprika Steak and Mushrooms (Cal 190, p.66)
Lunch 4.5 Falafel Patties (Cal 445, p.31)
Snack 12.10 Fragrant Onion Pakora (Cal 190, p.82)
Dinner 3.10 Air Fryer Scallops (Cal 500, p.25)
Nutrition Per Day:
Calories – 1770 | Fat - 43g | Carbs - 91g | Protein - 41g | Sugar – 8g | Fiber – 12.1g | Potassium - 1425mg | Sodium – 1810mg | Cholesterol – 415mg

Thursday
Breakfast 2.6 "Spanish" Frittata (Cal 460, p.13)
Snack 9.9 Beef Enchiladas (Cal 546, p.67)
Lunch 4.6 Mushroom Pasta (Cal 450, p.31)
Snack 12.11 Bacon and Balsamic Sprouts (Cal 100, p.83)
Dinner 3.11 Air Fryer Mussels (Cal 332, p.26)
Nutrition Per Day:
Calories – 1888 | Fat - 55g | Carbs - 124g | Protein - 37g | Sugar – 19g | Fiber – 17.3g | Potassium - 1175mg | Sodium – 2080mg | Cholesterol – 384mg

Friday
Breakfast 2.7 Ham & Egg Bites (Cal 450, p.14)
Snack 9.10 Spicy Steak Wraps (Cal 220, p.67)
Lunch 4.7 Courgette Rolls (Cal 400, p.32)
Snack 12.12 Cheesy, Garlic Asparagus (Cal 296, p.83)
Dinner 3.12 Boozy Fish Tacos (Cal 332, p.26)
Nutrition Per Day:
Calories – 1698 | Fat - 37g | Carbs - 104g | Protein - 43g | Sugar – 19g | Fiber – 14.6g | Potassium - 1127mg | Sodium – 1890mg | Cholesterol – 523mg

Saturday
Breakfast 2.8 Vegetable Hash Browns (Cal 400, p.14)
Snack 9.1 Steak and Asparagus Cubes (Cal 486, p.63)
Lunch 4.8 Cheese and Pasta Quiche (Cal 440, p.32)
Snack 12.13 Spicy Corn on The Cob (Cal 196, p.84)
Dinner 3.13 Herby Tilapia (Cal 650, p.27)
Nutrition Per Day:
Calories – 2172 | Fat - 72g | Carbs - 121g | Protein - 41g | Sugar – 9g| Fiber – 14g | Potassium - 1005mg | Sodium – 1710mg | Cholesterol – 252mg

Sunday

Breakfast 2.10 Full & Healthy Peppers (Cal 450, p.15)
Snack 9.3 Beef Wellington (Cal 256, p.64)
Lunch 4.10 Air Fryer Vegetable Bake (Cal 400, p.33)
Snack 12.15 Eggplant Snacks (Cal 200, p.85)
Dinner 3.15 Coconut Shrimp (Cal 630, p.28)
Nutrition Per Day:
Calories – 1932 | Fat - 64g | Carbs - 113g | Protein - 50g | Sugar – 12g | Fiber – 14.5g | Potassium - 1270mg | Sodium – 1400mg | Cholesterol – 987mg

13 ANALYTICAL INDEX

A

Air Fryer Dill Pickles 87
Air Fryer Eggs 11
Air Fryer Mussels 26
Air Fryer Omelet 15
Air Fryer Pierogies 38
Air Fryer Potatoes with Chicken 51
Air Fryer Ravioli 30
Air Fryer Scallops 25
Air Fryer Tofu 35
Air Fryer Vegetable Bake 33
Artichoke & Pumpkin Seed Pasta 37
Asian Fish Patties 23
Aubergine Parmesan 29
Avocado Chips 47

B

Bacon & Balsamic Sprouts 83
Banana & Walnut Bread 77
BBQ Ribs 59
BBQ Soy Curls 43
Beef Enchiladas 67
Beef Fried Rice 65
Beef Wellington 64
Boozy Fish Tacos 26
Breaded Pork Chops 58
Breakfast Pockets 18
Breakfast Sandwich 17

C

Canarian Potatoes 40
Cayenne Wings 55
Cheese & Ham in Puff Pastry 13
Cheese & Pasta Quiche 32
Cheese Tikka 30
Cheesy Bagel Pizza 41
Cheesy Baked Potato 42
Cheesy Carrot Chips 45
Cheesy Carrot Mushrooms 81
Cheesy Garlic Bread 78
Cheesy Lamb Balls 70
Cheesy Toast 16
Cheesy, Garlic Asparagus 83
Cherry Parcels 74
Chicken & Bacon BBQ Bites 78
Chicken & Jalapeño Chimichangas 56
Chicken Fried Rice 54
Chicken Thighs in Bacon 53
Chicken with a Bang! 53
Chinese Spiced Pork 61
Chinese Spring Rolls 81

Chocolate Soufflé 76
Citrus Cauliflower 29
Classic Apple Pie 75
Classic Chocolate Cake 76
Classic Creamy Cheesecake 75
Classic Lamb Patties 68
Coconut Asian Beef 64
Coconut Shrimp 28
Courgette & Coriander Burgers 39
Courgette Rolls 32
Crab Stuffed Mushrooms 21
Creamy Breakfast Treats 20
Creamy Pasta Bake 35
Crostini with Artichoke 42
Crunchy Ranch Potatoes 45

D

Delicious Profiteroles 74

E

Easy Boiled Eggs 19
Easy Bread crumbed Fish 22
Easy Chicken Nuggets 55
Easy Pancakes 12
Egg "Sandwiches" 20
Eggplant Snacks 85

F

Falafel Patties 31
Feta Hamburgers 65
Fish Taco Bowls 25
Fragrant Onion Pakora 82
French Toast 11
Fruity Balsamic Pork Chops 60
Fruity Tofu 48
Full & Healthy Peppers 15

G

Garlic Asparagus 46

H

Ham & Egg Bites 14
Healthy Vegetarian Pizza 34
Herby Tilapia 27
Honey & Apple Pasties 77

J

Jackfruit Taquitos 37
Jalapeño & Cream Cheese Pops 82

L

Lamb & Ginger Burgers 70

Lamb & Jalapeño Empanadas 69
Lamb & Parsley Roll 72
Lamb & Worcestershire Sauce Peppers 68
Lamb Kebabs 69
Lasagna Taco Bake 72
Lentil & Cabbage Patties 39
Lentil Balls 33

M

Marinated Cauliflower 49
Mediterranean Gnocchi 34
Mexican Steak & Chips 63
Morning Wraps 12
Mushroom & Onion "Pasties" 71
Mushroom Pasta 31

O

Onion Arancini 43
Onion Bhajis 79
Orange Cocoa Dip 73

P

Paprika & Garlic Chicken 56
Paprika Hash 19
Paprika Steak and Mushrooms 66
Parsley Courgette 48
Parsley Snack Potatoes 84
Picnic Scotch Eggs 80
Pineapple Pork 61
Pork & Ginger Meatballs 62
Pork & Marinara Sub 59
Pork Schnitzel 60
Pork Tenderloin in Dijon Mustard 58
Potato Gratin 36
Potatoes with Spinach 86
Pumpkin & Lemon Pasta 41

Q

Quick Morning Doughnuts 17

R

Radish Browns 38

S

Salmon Burgers 24
Sausage Surprise 16
Seasoned Belly Pork 62
Shrimp Pops 21
Simple Fish Fingers 23
Smoked Chicken 52
Snack Chickpeas 85
Spanish" Frittata 13
Spicy Corn on The Cob 84
Spicy Lamb Meatloaf 71
Spicy Pork Bites 79
Spicy Rice 46
Spicy Shrimp Boil 24
Spicy Steak Wraps 67
Spicy Tandoori Chicken 51
Spinach & Eggs 18
Steak & Asparagus Cubes 63
Sticky Chicken Thighs 54
Stringy Mozzarella Sticks 80
Stuffed Peppers with Beef 66
Stuffed Pumpkin 49
Sweet Potato Wraps 44

T

Tartar Battered Fish Sticks 27
Tasty Potato Wedges 47
Turkey and Mushroom Burgers 52
Turkey Bites 57
Turkey in Mushroom Sauce 50

V

Vanilla Biscuits 73
Vegan Cheese with Bread Sticks 40
Vegetable Hash Browns 14

Z

Zingy Lemon Chicken Wings 50
Zingy Shishito Peppers 86
Zingy Shrimp 22
Zucchini Snack Gratin 87

14 CONCLUSION

The hope is that by this point, you're feeling completely inspired and you're ready to start creating delicious meals with your air fryer. You'll also be more confident because you know it's not as hard as you first thought. All that's left to do is get started. These recipes give you a wide range of choices and you might be spoiled in terms of which one to opt for first. Take your time and follow all instructions. You'll quickly see how much potential your air fryer actually has. Without the need to order takeaways or make high fat foods, you'll feel healthier, and you'll probably feel far less sluggish as a result. You'll be able to make fantastic meals for all the family and even host dinner parties for your friends, using just your air fryer to wow them!

You can work your way through the recipes, or you can choose a random recipe and start with that. Simply go with whatever option makes sense to you and whatever draws you. As long as you follow instructions, you'll have delicious food to serve, and it will be on par with a restaurant in terms of crispiness and freshness. All that's left for us to do is wish you luck. Gain confidence using your air fryer by familiarizing yourself with it beforehand. Then, there'll be no stopping you!

15 BONUS

Scanning the following QR code will take you to a web page where you can access 9 fantastic bonuses after leaving your email and an honest review of my book on Amazon: 1 video course, 3 mobile apps and 4 guides about air fryer.

LINK: https://dl.bookfunnel.com/8kfdaj60bk

16 ANNEX – A

SHOPPING LIST FOR A WEEK OF DIET

FOOD ITEMS	QUANTITIES
Bread (for French Toast)	1 loaf
Eggs (for multiple recipes)	2 dozen
Potatoes (for various potato dishes)	5 lb. (2268g)
Aubergine (Eggplant)	2 large
Lamb (for various lamb dishes)	5 lb. (2268g)
Shrimp	1 lb. (453g)
Carrots (for carrot chips)	2 lb. (906g)
Bell peppers	6
Crab meat (for stuffed mushrooms)	1 lb. (453g)
Mushrooms	1 lb. (453g)
Pancake mix or ingredients	1 pack or equivalent
Rice (for spicy rice)	2 lb. (906g)
Cheese (for various recipes)	3 lb. (1361g)
Jalapenos	10-12
Fish (various types)	5 lb. (2268g)
Asparagus	1 lb. (453g)
Ravioli	2 packs
Puff pastry	2 packs
Falafel mix or ingredients	1 pack or equivalent
Ginger	1 small root
Avocado	6
Pasta (for mushroom pasta)	1 lb. (453g)
Tofu	1 lb. (453g)
Courgette (Zucchini)	5-6
Worcestershire Sauce	1 bottle

17 ANNEX - B

WASHING AND HANDLING

Importance of Proper Cleaning

Before delving into the intricacies of plant-based cooking, it's crucial to understand the importance of thoroughly washing fruits and vegetables. Doing so removes dirt, bacteria, and any pesticide residues, ensuring that your dishes are not only delicious but also safe to eat.

Step-by-Step Guide to Washing Produce

1. **Hand Hygiene:** First and foremost, before and after you prepare any fruits or vegetables, wash your hands thoroughly for at least 15-20 seconds using warm water and hand soap. This crucial step minimizes the transfer of bacteria to your food.
2. **Prepare Vinegar and Salt Solution:** Combine 1 1/3 cup of vinegar and 1 tablespoon of salt in a large bowl. Stir the mixture until both the vinegar and salt have completely dissolved. The vinegar serves as a natural disinfectant, while the salt aids in drawing out hidden microbes.
3. **Initial Rinse:** Fruits and vegetables should be initially rinsed under running water. It's essential to gently rub the surface to loosen dirt and any lingering pesticides. Avoid using soap or chemical cleansers as these can leave residues that are harmful if ingested.
4. **Soaking:** Different types of produce require different soaking times. For thin-skinned fruits and vegetables like berries and leafy greens, a 5-minute soak in the vinegar and salt solution is sufficient. Firm-skinned produce like apples and squash should be left in the solution for about 10 minutes. This step is critical for thorough disinfection.
5. **Scrubbing:** For hard and textured fruits or vegetables like melons, carrots, sweet potatoes, and cucumbers, utilize a clean vegetable brush to scrub their skins gently. This removes trapped dirt and microbes that a simple rinse may not eliminate.
6. **Rinsing Post-Soak:** After soaking and scrubbing, rinse the produce under running plain water to remove any lingering vinegar or salt. Make sure to rinse thoroughly to ensure that no residues are left behind.
7. **Drying:** Use a clean kitchen cloth or paper towel to dry the fruits and vegetables. This step is more than just for convenience; it further minimizes the chance of bacterial growth.
8. **Inspect and Cut:** Finally, inspect your produce for any damaged or bruised areas. Cut these away as they can harbor bacteria and negatively affect the quality and safety of your food. Designate separate cutting boards for fruits/vegetables and raw meats. Always wash boards with hot soapy water after use.
9. **Meat:** Wash hands, meat, and utensils with soap and hot water to prevent cross-contamination, then pat meat dry before seasoning or cooking. Follow proper cooking temperatures and times to ensure meat is safely prepared and cooked to the recommended internal temperature.

Extra Tips

- Leafy Greens: For leafy greens like kale and spinach, a salad spinner can be incredibly useful to remove excess water post-washing.
- Berry Care: Berries are delicate. Rinse them only before you're about to use them to prevent spoilage.
- Storing: Some fruits and vegetables like tomatoes and avocados should be stored at room temperature until they ripen; then, they can be refrigerated.

Remember, clean produce contributes to safe and delicious meals!

18 FAQS

Why should I use an air fryer instead of traditional frying?
Using an air fryer reduces the amount of oil used, making dishes healthier with fewer calories and less fat.

Is preheating the air fryer necessary?
While some recipes might not require preheating, it's often recommended for consistent and quicker cooking results.

How do I clean my air fryer?
Most air fryer parts are dishwasher safe. For manual cleaning, let the appliance cool, then wipe the inside with a damp cloth and wash the removable parts.

Can I stack food in the air fryer?
It's best not to stack food, as this can prevent even cooking. However, some models come with layering accessories.

How much food can I cook at once?
This depends on the size of your air fryer. Ensure that there's enough space for hot air to circulate freely around the food.

Is it possible to check food in mid-cooking?
Yes, you can pull out the basket to check, shake, or turn the food, then continue cooking.

Do I need to use oil in the air fryer?
While many recipes require little to no oil, a light spray can help achieve a crispy finish.

Can I cook frozen foods in the air fryer?
Absolutely! Just ensure you adjust the cooking time as needed.

Are there foods I shouldn't cook in an air fryer?
Delicate foods that can easily get blown around by the air fryer's fan, like lightweight pastries, might not be ideal.

How do I avoid smoke in my air fryer?
Ensure you don't overfill the oil or use high-fat content foods, and regularly clean your appliance to prevent residue buildup.

Why is my food not getting crispy?
Overcrowding or not using any oil at all can affect crispiness. Adjust accordingly.

What types of containers can I use inside my air fryer?
Always use oven-safe containers. Avoid plastic or anything that might melt or warp.

Is it normal for the air fryer to emit a smell when new?
Yes, a slight smell is typical during the first few uses but should dissipate over time.

Do I need to shake or turn the food while cooking?
For even cooking, many recipes recommend shaking or turning halfway through.

How long will it take for my food to cook in the air fryer?
Cooking times vary based on the recipe and food type. Refer to the "AIRFRYER COOKBOOK" for specific timings.

What's the ideal temperature for cooking most dishes?
Temperatures can range from 350°F to 400°F for many recipes, but always refer to the specific recipe for guidance.

Can I add seasonings or marinades to foods in the air fryer?
Absolutely! Just ensure excess marinade is drained to prevent smoking or splattering.

19 MEASUREMENTS

Volume Equivalents (Dry)	
US STANDARD	METRIC (APPROX.)
1/8 teaspoon	0.5 mL
1/4 teaspoon	1 mL
1/2 teaspoon	2 mL
3/4 teaspoon	4 mL
1 teaspoon	5 mL
1 tablespoon	15 mL
1/4 cup	59 mL
1/2 cup	118 mL
3/4 cup	177 mL
1 cup	235 mL
2 cups	475 mL
3 cups	700 mL
4 cups	1 L

Temperature Equivalents	
FAHR. (F)	METRIC (APPROX.)
225 °F	107 °C
250 °F	120 °C
275 °F	135 °C
300 °F	150 °C
325 °F	160 °C
350 °F	180 °C
375 °F	190 °C
400 °F	205 °C
425 °F	220 °C
450 °F	235 °C
475 °F	245 °C
500 °F	260 °C

Volume Equivalents (Liquid)		
US STANDARD	US STANDARD (OUNCES)	METRIC (APPROX.)
2 tablespoons	1 fl. oz.	30 mL
1/4 cup	2 fl. oz.	60 mL
1/2 cup	4 fl. oz.	120 mL
1 cup	8 fl. oz.	240 mL
1 1/2 cup	12 fl. oz.	355 mL
2 cups or 1 pint	16 fl. oz.	475 mL
4 cups or 1 quart	32 fl. oz.	1 L
1 gallon	128 fl. oz.	4 L

Weight Equivalents	
US STANDARD	METRIC (APPROXIMATE)
1 ounce	28 g
2 ounces	57 g
5 ounces	142 g
10 ounces	284 g
15 ounces	425 g
16 ounces (1 pound)	455 g
1.5 pounds	680 g
2 pounds	907 g

Printed in the USA
CPSIA information can be obtained
at www.ICGtesting.com
LVHW080149080924
790238LV00015B/1438